YESHUA
LAMB OF THE FIRST YEAR

With the Gospel of John

In chronological order from the ***B'rit HaChidaysh***

בְּרִית הָחֳדֵשׁ

"Covenant the Renewed"

Aka, The New Testament

This translation conforms as closely as possible to Biblical Hebrew

By Leonard Rothenberger, Jr

Published by Pesach Lamb Ministries

YESHUA, Lamb of the First Year

Rothenberger, Leonard Jr.

Copyright 2015

Published by Pesach Lamb Ministries

PO Box 2108

Canon City, CO 81215

info@PESACHLAMB.COM

PESACHLAMB.COM

ISBN 978-0-9961174-1-8

First edition

Cover design by Jenny Anderson, ebookcovers4u.com

(License notes) ALL RIGHTS RESERVED. This book contains material protected under International and Federal Copyright Laws and Treaties. Any unauthorized reprint or use of this material is prohibited. No part of this book may be reproduced or transmitted in any form or by any means, electronic or mechanical, including photocopying, recording, or by any information storage and retrieval system without express written permission from the author / publisher.

About the Cover

YESHUA as the *Pesach* Lamb had to be inspected for four days. The *Pesach* Lamb was brought into the home so it could be inspected. YESHUA rode into *Yerushalayim* on an ass's colt on the tenth of *Nisan*, the Biblical first day of the week aka Palm Sunday. YESHUA came to His FATHER'S HOUSE and was inspected for four days. It is stated in the Gospels that YESHUA taught daily in the TEMPLE after this entry into *Yerushalayim*.

The two goats: one represents *YESHUA* SON of My FATHER (*YESHUA BEN-ABBA*) and the other goat represents *Yeshua* son of my father (*Yeshua bar-Abba*) aka Barabbas. These two goats are provided from the Assembly and lots were placed before the foundation of the world was laid; like *Yom Kippur*, lots were place to determine which one is offered to *YAHVEH* and the other goat is sent into the wilderness for *Azazel*. This sacrifice is normally done at *Yom Kippur* also known as the Day of Atonement; but, this is not a normal Passover.

Acknowledgement

I would like to dedicate this book to my late wife Marilyn of 33 years, she was a major part of this journey. She went to be with our LORD YESHUA on March 24, 2013 after her second bout with cancer.

Marilyn and I are grateful to John (Dutch) and Rita Wiedeman for their friendship of 30 plus years. Dutch and Rita attend Anshey HaShem (People of the Name) in Canon City, Colorado where Dutch is assistant Rabbi.

Marilyn and I became acquainted with Dutch and Rita after we bought a house across the street from them in Gervais, Oregon. Marilyn started going to their church and I followed shortly after. Dutch and Rita moved around from state to state and finally settled in Canon City in 2003. Before settling in Canon City, they started learning about the Jewishness of the Bible and shared with Marilyn and Me.

In 2006 Marilyn and I took a trip to visit Dutch, Rita, and Anshey HaShem; 1400 miles one way from Oregon. We both enjoyed our visit and were considering moving to Colorado to join Dutch and Rita at Anshey HaShem. After we got back to Oregon, Dutch called and stated that the Rabbi said "they belong here". The following year by the end of September we finished moving to Canon City, Colorado.

I also want to thank Rabbi Robert Hansen and his wife Juanita for their fellowship, teachings, and times of worship. Marilyn and I have studied the Hebrew language with Juanita as our teacher. One day Juanita came up to me and said "we have no cantor today, would you mind filling-in?" Shortly after that, Marilyn said to me "we have no cantor," I said yes we do! No practice, just cold turkey; thank you Juanita; I was put on rotation from then on.

The research for this book got started when Dutch asked the question "where is the proof in scripture that YESHUA'S Ministry was only for **one** year?" I like a challenge; so the search was on.

Foreword

My wife, Rita, and I first met Leonard and Marilyn Rothenberger in 1981.

We were living in Gervais, Oregon at the time and observed a new family moving in across the street. A few days later we met the new family.

As we got to know Leonard and Marilyn better, Rita and Marilyn became good friends and I was amazed at how much knowledge Leonard had concerning a variety of things. Leonard is a welder by trade but had good working knowledge of tool making, electricity, plumbing, home repair, home building, etc. He was a real jack of all trades, quite the DIYer.

Leonard and Marilyn had a nice family and we were becoming very good friends. But they had one major defect. They didn't know, *Yeshua,* as Savior and Lord of their lives.

That began to change as Rita would talk to Marilyn about the Bible and her friend started going to church and taking the children as well. Leonard refused to go. His famous last words were, "You'll never get me in Church." But GOD, had His own plan, will and purpose for Leonards' life.

One day, I believe it was in the garage, Leonard committed his life to, *Yeshua*. Although we called Him Jesus then.

Leonard began to read the Bible as every believer should. He later began to study to put the salvation he was experiencing on a firm foundation.

As the years have gone by I have been amazed at how Leonards' knowledge of scripture has grown.

In February 2001, after studying, teaching and preaching in the Church for over forty-two years I was introduced to the Hebrew perspective of scripture. It wasn't long before I begin to share some of the teachings with Leonard. He would take the teaching and study it. Later he would get back with me and say".....you're right, and here's what else I found."

Thus, Leonard's journey into *Judaism* began.

Through the last twelve years he has not only studied *Torah* but also *Talmud* and come up with his own time-line of the *Messiah and this book* about the Messiahs ministry called '*Yeshua*, lamb of the first year'.

Many people who know Leonard have been amazed at how this study in *Judaism* has gotten into him so quickly. The truth is, through looking into his ancestry, Leonard found that he is an *Ashkenazi* Jew. The seed of Judaism was already there. All it needed was to be watered with the truth of *Torah* and cultivated with years of study.

As you read '*Yeshua,* lamb of the first year', may your heart be blessed with TRUTH. Amen

John L Wiedeman

TABLE OF CONTENTS

About the cover 5
Acknowledgement 6
Foreword 8
PREFACE 13
YESHUA Lamb of the First Year 15
   YESHUA'S Conception, Birth, and Ministry 15
Biblical Calendar with *YAHVEH'S* Appointed Times 25
Passover *Seder* to Resurrection 31
YESHUA Lamb of the First Year 39
John 41
Passover *Seder* 98
The Gospel of John 130
First Writing of John 131
Second Writing of John 139
Third Writing of John 161
Passover *Seder* 189
GLOSSARY 221
References 229
About the Author 230

PREFACE

YESHUA
Lamb of the first year

With the Gospel of John in chronological order. Why John? John mentions Passover three times; Matthew, Mark, and Luke mentions Passover one time. John is one witness used against many. How many witnesses are required in Biblical Law?

Commentaries, Theologians, Rabbis, and Pastors have mixed opinions and thought on how long *YESHUA'S* Ministry was; most say three to three and half years. You may ask, does it matter? So ask yourself, does your salvation matter? Does it matter what your salvation is based on or who it is based on? This may not be a salvation issue; but, this is an issue of the qualifications of the identity that your salvation is based on.

YESHUA'S Ministry, how long was it? Three years? Three and half years? One year? Or less than one year? Does it matter? What does *TORAH* say? Did *YESHUA* meet the qualifications to be our Passover Lamb by Biblical Law? And what are these qualifications?

YESHUA'S conception and birth, at random, or do they fit into "*YAHVEH'S Appointed Times*"?

Did The High Priest obtain his position according to Biblical Law, and did he perform his duties according to those Laws.

Is *YESHUA* mentioned in the "Old Testament"?

These questions need to be answered by two or three witnesses!

The Gospel of John was put in this order based on *YAHVEH'S Appointed Times*. John's Gospel is the only one that mentions all of *YAHVEH'S Appointed Times*; the other Gospels only mention Passover.

YESHUA
LAMB OF THE FIRST YEAR

YESHUA'S Conception, Birth, and Ministry

Luke 1:24 …"Elisabeth his wife conceived, and she remained **five months** in seclusion … 26 **In the sixth month (*Elul*),** the angel Gabriel was sent by *ELOHIM* to a city in Galilee called Nazareth, 27 to a virgin engaged to a man named Joseph, of the House of David; the virgin's name was Mary. 28 Approaching her, the angel said, 'Peace, favored lady! *ADONAI* is with you!' 29 She was deeply troubled by his words and wondered what kind of greeting this might be. 30 The angel said to her, 'Do not be afraid, Mary, for you have found favor with *ELOHIM*. 31 Look! You **will** become pregnant, you **will** give birth to a SON, and you are to name him *YESHUA*. 32 He will be great, He will be called SON of the Most High… 35 …The HOLY SPIRIT **will** come over you, the power of the Most High **will** cover you. Therefore the Holy Child born to you will be called the SON of *ELOHIM*. 36 You have a relative,

Elisabeth, who is an old woman; and everyone says she is barren. But she has conceived a son and is **six months** pregnant!' … 39 Without delay, Mary set out and hurried to the town in the hill country of Judea 40 where Zechariah lived, entered the house and greeted Elisabeth. 41 When Elisabeth heard Mary's greeting, the baby in her womb stirred. Elisabeth was filled with the HOLY SPIRIT 42 and spoke up in a loud voice, 'How blessed are you among women! And how blessed is the **Child** in your womb!'"

From verse Luke 1:24 through verse 36 one month has elapsed which would bring us to the **seventh month**, the month of *Tishri*. YESHUA was conceived in the month of *Tishri* (the 7th month) at *Rosh HaShanah*/Feast of *Shofars*" and was born nine months later in the third month of *Sivan* the same year at *Shavu'ot* aka "Pentecost" the giving of the *TORAH* on Mount Sinai. Genesis 41:36 Joseph, Son of Jacob was conceived also at *Rosh HaShanah* and starts his ministry at age thirty at *Shavu'ot*. Joseph is a fore runner of *YESHUA* SON of Joseph, the SERVANT MESSIAH.

Review

Elisabeth conceived in the first month, *Nisan*, Luke 1:24, 26, and 36.

John could have been born around *Chanukkah*, "Festival of Lights" at the end of the ninth month of *Kislev*. John will, Luke 1:76 **"…go before the LORD to prepare His way."**

In the sixth month (***Elul***) the angel Gabriel visited Mary, Luke 1:26. "The HOLY SPIRIT will come over you..." Luke 1:35. In the **future**.

Elisabeth is six months pregnant, Luke 1:36; (we are still in the sixth month of *Elul*.)

After this, (at the beginning of the seventh month, *Tishri*, Luke 1:42, Mary is with child. *Tishri* begins with *Rosh HaShanah* and the Feast of Shofars, and would put His birth at *Shavu'ot*.

At the Age of Twelve

Luke 2:41-42, *YESHUA* SON of Joseph was at *Yerushalayim* for the feast of Passover/Unleavened Bread at the age of twelve. *YESHUA*, staying behind in *Yerushalayim* after the festival was over as His parents were returning home, He made this statement to His parents when they returned and found Him in the TEMPLE Court in Luke 2:49…"Why did you have to look for Me? Did not you know that I had to be concerning Myself with My FATHER'S Affairs?" *YESHUA* returned home and was subject to His parents. [He would have been trained in His Father's trade as well as learned *TORAH*.]

Sometime after this event YESHUA left *Yerushalayim* and went to *Qumran* (this is where the sect of Judaism called the *Essenes* lived) where YESHUA and John went to a *yeshivah* and became "*Rabbis*" (*rabbi* means teacher.) John 1:38, "They said to Him," "*RABBI!*" 1:49; "Nathanael said," "*RABBI…*" 3:1-2 …Pharisees, named Nicodemus... This man came to *YESHUA* by night and said to Him, "*RABBI…*" (3:26, John was also a called a "*Rabbi*" by his disciples and a Jew.) John 6:25, some of the crowd that were part of the five thousand fed the previous day called Him "***RABBI.***"

YESHUA becomes the PASSOVER LAMB

From Luke 2:41-42 above fast forward approximately seventeen years to Luke 3:1-2, John, Son of Zechariah, (at the age of 30) began witnessing *immersions* around the Jordan. (John, Son of Zechariah was six months older than *YESHUA*, Luke 1:8-25, 26-38.) It is my belief that *YESHUA* returned to *Yerushalayim* around the time of the Passover/Unleavened Bread festival; which is the first of three *pilgrimage feasts* called "*YAHVEH'S Appointed Times*" Leviticus 23:2; and then went to the Jordan to have His *Immersion* witnessed by John the *Immerser* during the festival of Passover/Unleavened

Bread; Matthew 3:13 **"Then *YESHUA* came from the Galilee to the Jordan to be *immersed* by John.** (This could have been on *First Fruits*, which is on the "first day of the week" following the first day of Unleavened Bread and the day that *YESHUA* eventually rose from the grave.) As stated in the *TORAH* that the "Passover Lamb" has to be a lamb in its first year; Exodus 12:5 **"An unblemished lamb or kid, a male, within its first year shall it be for you…"** *YESHUA* became the "PASSOVER LAMB" at His *Immersion* witnessed by John. In another words, this is when the "PASSOVER LAMB" is born, *YESHUA* **was born again**, **the start of His year.** I believe that His *Immersion* was during the festival of Unleavened Bread and most likely on *"First Fruits"*, which would have been on the 17th or later of *Nisan*. (*YESHUA* was crucified on the fourteenth of *Nisan* the following year; making His Ministry less than one year at this point in time.) *YESHUA* was led into the wilderness for 40 days and nights then returned to *Yerushalayim* for the feast of *Shavu'ot*. During the feast of *Shavu'ot*, *YESHUA* turns 30 years old and starts His Ministry as PROPHET and PRIEST. *YESHUA* met the requirements at this time for the priesthood in Numbers 4:3 **"from thirty years of age and up…"** *YESHUA* started selecting His Disciples at this time.

John and *YESHUA* were cousins and most likely went to a *yeshivah* together. So prior to *YESHUA'S Immersion*, He was not "*ELOHIM'S* LAMB;" even though He is the LAMB slain before the foundation of the world, Revelation 13:8.

Thus, John the *Immerser* did not know who *YESHUA* was as far as *YESHUA* being the "Passover Lamb" prior to His *Immersion*. John states this fact twice, John 1:31. "**I myself did not know who He was**, but the reason I came *immersing* with Water was so that He might be made known to *Yisrael*." 32 Then John gave this testimony: "I saw the SPIRIT coming down from heaven like a Dove, and remaining on Him. 33 **I myself did not know who He was**, but the One who sent me to *immerse* in Water said to me, 'The One on whom you see the Spirit descending and remaining, this is the One who *immerses* in the HOLY SPIRIT.' 34 And I have seen and borne witness that this is the SON of *ELOHIM*."

YESHUA makes a statement about being **"born again."** John 3:1, there was a man among the Pharisees, named Nicodemus, who was a ruler of the Jews. 2 This man came to *YESHUA* by night and said to Him, "*RABBI*, we know it is from *ELOHIM* that You have come as a Teacher; for no one can do these miracles You perform unless *ELOHIM* is with Him." 3 "Yes, indeed," *YESHUA* answered him, "I tell you that unless a person is **born again** from above, he cannot see the Kingdom of *ELOHIM*." 4 Nicodemus said to Him, "How can a grown man be 'Born'? Can he go back into his mother's womb and be born a second time?" 5 *YESHUA* answered, "Yes, indeed, I tell you that unless a person is **born** from Water and the SPIRIT, he cannot enter the Kingdom of *ELOHIM*. 6 What is born from the flesh is flesh, and what is **born** from the Spirit is Spirit. 7 Stop being amazed at My telling you that you must be **born again** from above! 8 The wind blows where it wants to, and you hear its sound, but you do not know where it comes from or where it is going. That is how it is with everyone who has been born from the SPIRIT."

2 Corinthians 5:17 "…he is a new creation…"

Galatians 6:15 "…what matters is being a new creation."

1 Peter 1:23 "You have been born again…"

After His *Immersion*, Matthew 4:1-2 **"Then the SPIRIT led *YESHUA* up into the wilderness to be tempted by the Adversary. After *YESHUA* had fasted forty days and nights…"** Luke 3:23 **"*YESHUA* about thirty years old when He began His public ministry."** Note: from the *TORAH* a priest starts his priestly duties at 30 years of age. Numbers 4:3-4, **"From thirty years of age and up, until fifty years of age,** everyone who comes to the legion to perform work in the Tent of Meeting." Numbers 4:23, 30, 35, 39, 43, 47 are similar.

YESHUA'S Ministry Starts – *Shavu'ot*

John the *Immerser* makes a comment twice to his disciples about *YESHUA* after *YESHUA'S* return from His time in the wilderness and most likely during the feast of *Shavu'ot*, referring to *YESHUA* as "*ELOHIM'S* LAMB," *YESHUA* just turned thirty years old at which time He can start His Priestly Ministry.

When *YESHUA* walked by John and his disciples, John replied - 1:29 **"…Look! *ELOHIM'S* LAMB!...** 36 **…Look! *ELOHIM'S* LAMB."** Two of John's disciples followed *YESHUA*, and *YESHUA* said to them **"What seek ye?"** They said to Him, **"RABBI!"**

It is my opinion that at this time *YESHUA* had been spending time at *Yerushalayim* during the Feast of *Shavu'ot;* a pilgrimage feast. *Shavu'ot* is when the *TORAH* was given to Moses, the *Yisraelites*, and a mixed multitude, Exodus 12:38. *YESHUA*, according to the Gospel of Luke 1:24-42 was born on *Shavu'ot*; which would make Him thirty years old at this time and able to start His Priestly duties. On the day of *Shavu'ot YESHUA* starts to come in contact with His Disciples, starting with Andrew the brother of Simon Peter, John 1:40. Next was Simon Son of John known as Peter verse 42, Philip verse 43, and Nathanael verse 45.

Not until John the *Immerser* was in prison; according to the Gospel of Matthew; did *YESHUA* start His public ministry; Matthew 4:12 **"When *YESHUA* heard that John had been put in prison… 4:17 From that time on, *YESHUA* began proclaiming, "'Turn from your sins to *ELOHIM*, for the Kingdom of Heaven is near!'"** Matthew 11:2-3 **"Meanwhile, John the *Immerser*, who had been put in prison, heard what the Messiah had been doing; so he sent a message to Him through his disciples, asking, 'Are you the One who is to come, or should we look for someone else?'"**

For future study and discussion: continue above thought; "Are you the One who is to come, or should we look for someone else?" John knew that there would be two events; first event as *YESHUA* SON of Joseph and second event as *YESHUA* SON of David. This was *YESHUA'S* first event!

Review

YESHUA was "born again" as the PASSOVER LAMB on or

after the seventeenth of *Nisan*; fifty days later He turned thirty years old and able to start His Priestly Ministry; shortly after John is put in prison, then *YESHUA* starts proclaiming. Almost two months have passed and ten months to go till His Crucifixion. HIS Ministry was approximately ten months long.

YESHUA participated in only one *Preparation Day* for Passover after He started His Ministry. Remember He has to be **"A LAMB of the *FIRST YEAR*",** and *YESHUA* did not become this Lamb until His *Immersion* witnessed by John the *Immerser*.

BIBLICAL CALENDAR WITH *YAHVEH'S* APPOINTED TIMES

All months have 29 or 30 days

SPRING FEASTS

1st *Nisan* Preparation Day, *Pesach* Lamb slaughtered 14th; *Matzah* 15-21; *First Fruits* - Biblical 1st day of week after the 15th, which starts Saturday evening after sundown; and the start of "counting of the *Omer*," (50).

2nd *Iyar*

3rd *Sivan* *Shavu'ot* (Pentecost) 50 days after *First Fruits*

4th *Tammuz*

5th *Av*

6th *Elul*

FALL FEASTS

7ᵗʰ *Tishri* *Tishri* 1 & 2 *Rosh HaShanah** and Feast of Shofars; 10ᵗʰ *Yom Kippur* - Day of Atonement; 15-21 *Sukkot* - Feast of Booths/Tabernacle

8ᵗʰ *Cheshvan*

9ᵗʰ *Kislev* 25ᵗʰ *Chanukkah* - Feast of Dedication - Festival of Lights, 8 days (Tradition)

10ᵗʰ *Tevet*

11ᵗʰ *Shevat*

12ᵗʰ *Adar I*

13ᵗʰ *AdarII* In a leap year; seven leap years in a 19 year span.

*Rosh HaShanah (the day that no man knows the day nor hour) is celebrated for two days; it is the only feast day that starts with the sighting of the new moon. Matthew 24:36 "But when that day and hour come, no one knows…" Mark 13:32 "…when that day and hour come, no one knows…"

There are three Pilgrimage Feast in *YAHVEH'S Appointed Times*; that one, or a member of one's family is required to go up to *Yerushalayim*, and these are: *Pesach/Matzah*; *Shavu'ot*;

and *Sukkot*. The Sabbath is also an *Appointed Time*.

When months are mentioned by number (Nisan – Adar I or II), it is referring to the Biblical Calendar of *YAHVEH'S Appointed Times*. The month of *Tishri* begins with *Rosh HaShanah* which is the start of the Biblical New Year (*Tishri – Elul*) for the observance of the *Sabbatical* years and the *Jubilee*.

Qualifications of the PASSOVER LAMB

On the tenth of *Nisan*, YESHUA came to His FATHER'S HOUSE (The TEMPLE in *Yerushalayim*) to be examined until the fourteenth of *Nisan*.

Exodus 12:3-6 "...On the tenth of this month they shall take for themselves - each man - a lamb or kid for each fathers house... 5 An unblemished lamb or kid, a male, within its first year... 6 It shall be yours for examination until the fourteenth day of this month..."

Matthew 21:10-12 "When He entered *Yerushalayim*...12 "*YESHUA* entered the TEMPLE Grounds…"

Mark 11:11 "*YESHUA* entered *Yerushalayim*, went into the TEMPLE Courts…"

Luke 19:45 "Then *YESHUA* entered the TEMPLE Grounds…"

John 12:1, 12-13 1 "Six days before Passover… (9th); 12 The next day…into *Yerushalayim* (10th). 13 They took palm branches… 2:13…festival of Passover…up to *Yerushalayim*. 2:23 Now while *YESHUA* was in *Yerushalayim* at the Passover festival…"

Zechariah 9:9 "Rejoice greatly, O daughter of Zion Shout for joy, O daughter of *Yerushalayim*! For behold, your KING will come to you, righteous and victorious is He, a humble Man riding upon a donkey, upon a foal, a calf of she-donkeys." <u>The tenth of *Nisan*</u>.

Exodus 12:5 "An unblemished lamb or kid, male, within its first year…"

Hebrews 9:14 "…Messiah…offered Himself to *ELOHIM* as a sacrifice without blemish…"

1 Peter 1:19 "…death of the Messiah as of a Lamb without defect or spot." In the eyes of both Jews and Gentiles; Luke 23:4 Pilate said to the head Priests and the crowds, "I find no ground for a charge against this man."

Exodus 12:6a "It shall be your for examination until the fourteenth"

Matthew 26:2 "…Passover is two days away… 20 When

evening came, *YESHUA* reclined with the twelve…" (Dawning of the 14th.)

Mark 11:12 "The next day… 27 They went back into *Yerushalayim*…; 14:1 …two days before Passover; 17 When evening came…" (14th)

Luke 19:47 "Every day He taught at the TEMPLE. 22:7 Then came the day of Unleavened Bread, on which the Passover Lamb had to be killed." (14th)

John 13:2 "They were at supper…" (Dawning of the 14th.)

Exodus 12:6b "…*Yisrael* shall slaughter in the afternoon." (3:00 PM)

Deuteronomy 16:1-2 "…perform the Passover-offering… 2 You shall slaughter the Passover-offering…"

Matthew 26:46 "At about three…50… yielded up His Spirit."

Mark 15:25 "It was nine in the morning when they nailed Him to the *stake* 33 at noon… 34 At three…37…gave up His Spirit."

Luke 23:44 "It was about noon…until three o'clock in the afternoon… 46…He gave up His Spirit."

John 19:14 "…noon on *Preparation Day* for Passover (14th)… 30…He delivered up His Spirit."

Leviticus 23:5 "In the first month on the 14th of the month in the afternoon is the time of the Passover-offering to *ADONAI.*

Numbers 9:2-3 "...*Yisrael* shall make the Passover-offering in its appointed time. 3 On the fourteenth day of this month in the afternoon..."

Numbers 9:5 "They made the Passover-offering in the first month, on the fourteenth day of the month, in the afternoon... 28:16 In the first month, on the fourteenth day, shall be a Passover-offering to *ADONAI.*"

<u>**Exodus 12:14** "...as an eternal decree..."</u>

Luke 22:19 "...do this in memory of Me."

I Corinthians 11:24 ..."Do this as a memorial to Me." 25 ..."as a memorial to Me."

On the tenth of *Nisan,* YESHUA came to His FATHER'S HOUSE (The Temple in *Yerushalayim*) to be examined until the fourteenth of *Nisan.*

Passover *Seder* to Resurrection

YESHUA'S Passover *Seder*, what day?

Matthew 26:17-20 "On the first day of Unleavened Bread...20 When evening came..."

Mark 14:12-17 "On the first day of Unleavened Bread...17 When evening came..."

Luke 22:7-14 "Then came the day of Unleavened Bread...14 When the time came..."

John 13:1-2 "It was just before the festival of Passover...2 They were at supper..."

Wednesday evening (after sunset), *Nisan* 14.

YESHUA'S Death, what day?

Matthew 26:17-27:50, 27:1 "Early in the morning... 46 At about three... 50 ...yielded up His Spirit."

Mark 15:1-37, 15:1 "As soon as it was morning... 34 At three... 37 ...and gave up His Spirit."

Luke 22:1-23:46, 22:66 "At daybreak… 23:44…until three o'clock… 46…gave up His Spirit."

John 18:28-19:30 "They led *YESHUA* from Caiaphas to the governor's headquarters. By now it was early morning. They did not enter the headquarters building because they did not want to become ritually defiled and thus unable to eat the Passover meal…19:14 It was about noon on *Preparation Day* for Passover... 30 …He delivered up His Spirit. 31 It was *Preparation Day*…"

Thursdays afternoon at 3:00 PM, *Nisan* **14.**

YESHUA'S Burial, what day?

Matthew 27:57 "Towards evening…"

Mark 15:42 "Since it *Preparation Day*, as evening approached…"

Luke 23:50-55 54 "It was *Preparation Day*, and a Sabbath was about to begin. 55…they saw the tomb and how His Body was placed in it."

John 19:31-42 "It was *Preparation Day*, and the Jews did not want the bodies to remain on the *stake* on the Sabbath, since it was an especially important Sabbath. 42 So, it was *Preparation Day* for the Jews…they buried *YESHUA*."

Thursday evening before sunset, *Nisan* 14.

***YESHUA'S* Resurrection, what day?**

Matthew 28:1-6 "After Sabbath, as the next day was dawning... 6 He is not here, because He has been raised..."

Mark 16:1-6 "When Sabbath was over...2 Very early the next day, just after sunrise, they went to the tomb. 6 ...He has risen..."

Luke 24:1-6 "but the next day, while it was still very early...2 And found the stone rolled away...6 He is not here; He has been raised."

John 20:1 "Early on the *'first day of the* week', while it was still dark...and saw that the stone had been removed from the tomb."

The Biblical calendar "dawning of the day" starts in the evening; after sunset; after the sighting of three stars; approx. 7 PM, *Nisan* 17. So, the Biblical <u>First Day of the Week</u> starts at sundown Saturday evening. Not at midnight or sunrise.

Again, referring to John 20:1, The Sabbath day was over, the sun had set and Mary Magdalene saw the first three stars in the sky, "going-out of the Sabbath," and went to the tomb, approximately 7:00 PM Saturday.

Three days, three nights - Matthew 12:40 "For just as Jonah was three days and three nights in the belly of the sea-monster, so will the SON of Man be three days and three nights in the depths of the earth."

First Day	Thursday afternoon
First Night	Thursday evening into Friday
Second Day	Friday
Second Night	Friday evening into Saturday
Third Day	Saturday
Third Night	Saturday evening (not Sunday Morning)

Passover *Seder*, Death, Burial, and Resurrection

Read the Gospels of Matthew, Mark, Luke, and John and tell me what day of the week that *YESHUA* had His *Seder*, died, was buried, and arose from the grave. Do any of the Gospel writings line up with *TORAH*? Yes, one more than the others, the Gospel of John. The Passover *Seder*: only John; Death: John mentions the day; Burial: Mark, Luke, and John; Resurrection: Matthew and John.

More writings would be in order if the correct terminology was used and that there were no errors in our Bibles! For example, in the Bible "dawning of the day" would be at sunset, to the Gentile it is at sunrise. **Genesis 1:5 ...And there was evening and there was morning, one day;"** *ELOHIM* starts the day with evening. Part of a day equals the whole day; Matthew 20:1-16 Parable of the workers; those that worked half an hour got paid the same as those that worked all day. *Rabbi* John (Dutch) Wiedeman, "This is a Jewish book and needs to be understood with Jewish thought and intent." YESHUA is a Jew!

Three witnesses: Matthew, Mark, and Luke recount only one Passover, where one witness: John recounts the same Passover three times. Yet, John (as taught by most) is given higher status. Quoting *YESHUA* in John 8:17 "And even in your *Torah* it is **written that the testimony of two people is valid."** I Kings 21:10 "Then seat two unscrupulous people opposite him, who will testify against him..." ***TORAH*, Deuteronomy 17:6 "By the testimony of two witnesses or three witnesses..."** The three Passovers that John mentions are all one and the same. There are at least six witnesses that shows *YESHUA'S* Ministry to be less than one year - Matthew, Mark, Luke, and John when set in order, *TORAH*, and under Roman rule The High Priest was only in office for a year at a time; where as in the Biblical Priesthood, they could hold the position from thirty years of age to fifty. Caiaphas was The High Priest (Luke 3:1-3) when John started witnessing *immersions* and was The High Priest (John 18:13) when *YESHUA* was crucified.

For future study and discussion: *YESHUA* performed a second sacrifice at this time.

At *Yom Kippur* two goats are brought before the High Priest (Leviticus 16:5 **"from the assembly"**) and lots are placed. At the assembly before Pilate two were presented; *YESHUA BEN-ABBA* and *Yeshua bar-Abba* aka Barabbas; both were *Yeshua* son of my father. Leviticus 16:8 **"…one lot for *YAHVEH* and one lot for *Azazel*."** The first one was offered up as a sacrifice; the second one had the sins of the people place upon it and was lead out into the wilderness. The assembly made their choice; *YESHUA BEN-ABBA* was offered up to *ELOHIM* and *Yeshua bar-Abba* was led away to *Azazel*. Reference Leviticus 16:5, 7-10, 15-16, 18-22, 26-27.

YESHUA BEN-ABBA can only redeem kin: Matthew 10:6 "but go rather to the lost sheep of the House of *Yisrael*." Matthew 15:24 "He said, 'I was sent only to the lost sheep of the House of *Yisrael*.'" John 1:31 "...so that He might be made known to *Yisrael*." John 4:22 Quoting *YESHUA*, "...because salvation comes from the Jews."

Romans 11:17-24 is very important now; John 14:21 "Whoever has My Commands (*613*) and keeps them is the one who loves Me,..." 14:23 "...if someone loves Me, he will keep My WORD (*TORAH*)..." John 1:12 "But to as many as did receive Him, to those who put their faith in His Person and Power, <u>He gave the right to become Children of *ELOHIM*,...</u>" <u>What is required to earn the right to become Children of *ELOHIM*?</u> May it be John 14:21 and 23? Malachi 3:6 "**For I am the LORD, I change not...**" Proverbs 2:1a "My child, if you accept my words..." The conditional if, is to be understood as: "You will be my child if you accept my words" (Rashi).

Question: Did *Yeshua bar-Abba* (Barabbas) take the sins of the assembly to *Azazel* in the wilderness? The assembly was most likely a mixed multitude! And this sacrifice brought the Gentile within the kinship of *YESHUA*. The book of Ruth has more on kinsman redeemer.

The Bible is known to the Gentiles as the "Old Testament" and the "New Testament;" both are <u>new</u> to them. To the Jew, the *Tanakh* (Old Testament) contains the covenants and the *B'rit HaChidaysh* (New Testament) is a renewal of the covenants in the *Tanakh*. YESHUA, His Disciples, and the other writers of the New Testament did not have a New Testament; they quoted and studied the *Tanakh*.

Is *YESHUA* referred to in the "Old Testament"? Does the *Alpha* and *Omega* refer to *YESHUA*? *Alpha* and *Omega* are Greek letters; what would there Hebrew counter parts be? *Alef* and *Tav*, the first and last letters of the Hebrew alphabet. The *Alef/Tav* appears twice in Genesis 1:1 in the Hebrew text, and countless times after this. The *Alef/Tav* are <u>never</u> translated into English.

YESHUA
LAMB OF THE FIRST YEAR

With the Gospel of John

In chronological order from the **B'rit HaChidaysh**

בְּרִית הָחִדֶּשׁ

"Covenant the Renewed"

Aka The New Testament

This translations conforms as closely as possible to Biblical Hebrew

The Gospel of John is three separate writings

<u>First Writing</u>: John 1:1-2:25 *YESHUA'S* ministry ends at Passover. After John 2:13-23 Passover is not mentioned anymore; what happened to the crucifixion? Next festival

mentioned at 4:45; followed by the next at 5:1.

Second Writing: John 3:1-7:1; 6:71 Judah, Son of Simon from Iscariot…was soon to betray Him, at Passover.

Third Writing: John 7:2-21:25   But the festival of Tabernacle was near! What happened to Passover in the previous verse 6:71? **Passover (6:71) and Tabernacle (7:2) are six months apart.**

The parallel writings of Matthew, Mark, and Luke will be inserted where they match John; and marked with a shofar; also, where there is a break in sequence.

JOHN

1.1 In the beginning was the WORD/*TORAH*, and the WORD/*TORAH* was with *ELOHIM*, and the WORD/*TORAH* was *ELOHIM*. 2 He (*TORAH/YESHUA/*יהוה) was with *ELOHIM* in the beginning. 3 All things came to be through Him, and without Him nothing made had being. 4 In Him was Life, and the Life was the Light of mankind. 5 The Light shines in the darkness, and the darkness has not suppressed It.

6 There was a man sent from *ELOHIM* whose name was John. 7 He came to be a testimony, to bear witness concerning the Light; so that through Him, everyone might put his faith in *ELOHIM* and be faithful to Him. 8 He himself was not that Light; no, he came to bear witness concerning the Light.

9 This was the True Light, which gives Light to everyone entering the world. 10 He was in the world and the world came to be through Him; yet the world did not know Him. 11 He came to His Own Homeland, yet His Own People did not receive Him.

12 But to as many as did receive Him, to those who put their

faith in His Person and Power, He gave the right to become Children of *ELOHIM*, 13 not because of bloodline, physical impulse or human intention, but because of *ELOHIM*.

14 The WORD/*TORAH* became a human being and lived with us, and we saw His DIVINE PRESENCE, the DIVINE PRESENCE of the FATHER'S only SON, full of Grace and Truth.

15 John witnessed concerning Him when he cried out, "This is the Man I was talking about when I said, 'The One coming after me has come to rank ahead of me, because He existed before me.'"

16 We have all received from His Fullness, yes, Grace upon Grace. 17 For the *TORAH* was given through Moses; Grace and Truth came through *YESHUA* the MESSIAH.

18 No one has ever seen *ELOHIM*; but the Only and Unique SON, who is identical with *ELOHIM* and is at the FATHER'S Side; He has made The FATHER known.

19 Here is John's testimony: when the Jews sent Priest and Levites from *Yerushalayim* to ask him, "Who are you?" 20 He was very straightforward and stated clearly, "I am not the MESSIAH." 21 "Then who are you?" they asked him. "Are you Elijah?" "No, I am not," he said. "Are you 'the

PROPHET,' the One we're expecting?" "No," he replied. 22 So they said to him, "Who are you, so that we can give an answer to the people who sent us? What do you have to say about yourself?" 23 He answered in the words of the prophet, Isaiah 40:3 "I am **The voice of someone crying out: 'In the wilderness make the way of *ADONAI* straight!'"**

24 Some of those who had been sent were Pharisees. 25 They asked him, "If you are neither the MESSIAH nor Elijah nor 'the PROPHET,' then why are you *immersing* people?" 26 To them John replied, "I am *immersing* people in Water, but among you is standing Someone whom you do not know. 27 He is the One coming after me and I am not good enough even to untie His Sandal!" 28 All this took place in Bethlehem east of the Jordan, where John was *immersing*.

29 The next day, John saw *YESHUA* coming toward him and said, "Look! *ELOHIM'S* LAMB! The One who is taking away the sins of the world! 30 This is the Man I was talking about when I said, 'After me is coming Someone who has to rank above me, because He existed before me.' 31 I myself did not know who He was, but the reason I came *immersing* with Water was so that He might be made known to *Yisrael*." 32 Then John gave this testimony: "I saw the SPIRIT coming down from Heaven like a Dove, and remaining on Him. 33 I

myself did not know who He was, but the One who sent me to *immerse* in Water said to me, 'The One on whom you see the SPIRIT descending and remaining, this is the One who *immerses* in the HOLY SPIRIT.' 34 And I have seen and borne witness that this is the SON of *ELOHIM*." [*YESHUA* was "Born Again" at this time.]

35 The next day, John was again standing with two of his disciples. 36 On seeing *YESHUA* walking by, he said, "Look! *ELOHIM'S* LAMB!" 37 His two disciples heard him speaking, and they followed *YESHUA*. 38 *YESHUA* turned and saw them following Him, and He asked them, "What are you looking for?" They said to Him, "*RABBI*!" "Where are you staying?" 39 He said to them, "Come and see." So they went and saw where He was staying, and remained with Him the rest of the day; it was about four o'clock in the afternoon. 40 One of the two who had heard John and had followed *YESHUA* was Andrew the brother of Simon Peter.

41 The first thing he did was to find his brother Simon and tell him, "We have found the *MASHIACH*!" (The word means "One who has been Anointed.") 42 He took him to *YESHUA*. Looking at him, *YESHUA* said, "You are Simon, Son of John; you will be known as Peter." (The name means "rock.")

43 The next day, having decided to leave for the Galilee, *YESHUA* found Philip and said, "Follow Me!" 44 Philip was from Bethsaida, the town where Andrew and Peter lived. 45 Philip found Nathanael and told him, "We have found the One that Moses wrote about in the *TORAH*, also the Prophets, it is *YESHUA,* SON of Joseph from Nazareth!" 46 Nathanael answered him, "Nazareth? can anything good come from there?" "Come and see," Philip said to him. 47 *YESHUA* saw Nathanael coming toward Him and remarked about him, "Here is a true Son of *Yisrael*; nothing false in him!" 48 Nathanael said to Him, "How do You know me?" *YESHUA* answered him, "Before Philip called you, when you were under the fig tree, I saw you." 49 Nathanael said, "*RABBI,* you are the SON of *ELOHIM!* You are the King of *Yisrael!*" 50 *YESHUA* answered him, "You believe all this just because I told you I saw you under the fig tree? You will see greater things than that!" 51 Then He said to him, "Yes indeed! I tell you that you will see Genesis 28:12 **Heaven** opened and **the Angels of ELOHIM going up and coming down** on the SON of Man!"

2:1 On the third day of the week, there was a wedding at Cana in the Galilee; and the mother of *YESHUA* was there. 2 *YESHUA* too was invited to the wedding, along with His Disciples. 3 The wine ran out, and *YESHUA'S* Mother said to

Him, "They have no more wine." 4 *YESHUA* replied, "Mother, why should that concern Me? Or you? My time has not come yet." 5 His Mother said to the servants, "Do whatever He tells you." 6 Now six stone water-jars were standing there for the Jewish ceremonial washings, each with a capacity of twenty or thirty gallons. 7 *YESHUA* told them, "Fill the jars with water," and they filled them to the brim. 8 He said, "Now draw some out, and take it to the man in charge of the banquet;" and they took it. 9 The man in charge tasted the Water; it had now turned into wine! He did not know where it had come from, but the servants who had drawn the water knew. So he called the bridegroom 10 and said to him, "Everyone else serves the good wine first and the poorer wine after people have drunk freely. But you have kept the good wine until now!" 11 This, the first of *YESHUA'S* miraculous signs, He did at Cana in the Galilee; He manifested His Glory, and His Disciples came to have faith in Him. 12 Afterwards, He and His Mother and Brothers and His Disciples went down to Capernaum and stayed there a few days.

3:1 There was a man among the Pharisees, named Nicodemus, who was a ruler of the Jews. 2 This man came to *YESHUA* by night and said to Him, "*RABBI*, we know it is from *ELOHIM* that You have come as a Teacher; for no one can do these miracles You perform unless *ELOHIM* is with Him." 3 "Yes, indeed," *YESHUA* answered him, "I tell you that unless a person is born again from above, he cannot see the Kingdom of *ELOHIM*." 4 Nicodemus said to Him, "How can a grown man be 'born'? Can he go back into his mother's womb and be born a second time?" 5 *YESHUA* answered, "Yes, indeed, I tell you that unless a person is born from Living Water and the Spirit, he cannot enter the Kingdom of *ELOHIM*. 6 What is born from the flesh is flesh, and what is born from the Spirit is Spirit. 7 Stop being amazed at My telling you that you must be born again from above! 8 The wind blows where it wants to, and you hear its sound, but you do not know where it comes from or where it is going. That is how it is with everyone who has been born from the Spirit"

9 Nicodemus replied, "How can this happen?" 10 *YESHUA* answered him, "You hold the office of Teacher in *Yisrael*, and you do not know this? 11 Yes, indeed! I tell you that what we speak about, we know; and what we give evidence of, we have seen; but you people do not accept our evidence! 12 If you people do not believe Me when I tell you about the things of the world, how will you believe Me when I tell you about the

things of Heaven? 13 No one has gone up into Heaven; there is only the One who has come down from Heaven, the SON of Man. 14 Just as Moses lifted up the serpent in the wilderness, so must the SON of Man be lifted up; 15 so that everyone who has faith in Him may have Eternal Life.

16 "For *ELOHIM* so loved the world that He gave His Only and Unique SON, so that everyone who has faith in Him may have Eternal Life, instead of being utterly destroyed. 17 For *ELOHIM* did not send the SON into the world to judge the world, but rather so that through Him, the world might be saved. 18 Those who have faith in Him are not judged; those who do not have faith have been judged already, in that they have not trusted in the One who is *ELOHIM'S* Only and Unique SON. 19 "Now this is the judgment: the Light has come into the world, but people loved the darkness rather than the Light. Why? Because their actions were wicked. 20 For everyone who does evil things hates the Light and avoids It, so that his actions would not be exposed. 21 But everyone who does what is True comes to the Light, so that all may see that His actions are accomplished through *ELOHIM*."

7:2 But the festival of Tabernacles in Judea was near; 3 so His

Brothers said to Him, "Leave here and go into Judea, so that Your Disciples can see the miracles You do; 4 for no one who wants to become known acts in secret. If You are doing these things, show Yourself to the world!" 5 (His Brothers spoke this way because they had not put their faith in Him.) 6 *YESHUA* said to them, "My time has not yet come; but for you, any time is right. 7 The world cannot hate you, but it does hate Me, because I keep telling it how wicked its ways are. 8 You, go on up to the festival; as for Me, I Am not going up to this festival now, because the right time for Me has not yet come." 9 Having said this, He stayed on in the Galilee.

10 But after His Brothers had gone up to the festival, He too went up, not publicly but in secret. 11 At the festival, the Jews were looking for Him. "Where is He?" They asked. 12 And among the crowds there was much whispering about Him. Some said, "He is a good Man;" but others said, "No, He is deceiving the masses." 13 However, no one spoke about Him openly, for fear of the Jews.

14 Not until the festival was half over did *YESHUA* go up to the TEMPLE Courts and begin to teach. 15 The Jews were surprised: "How does this man know so much without having studied?" they asked. 16 So *YESHUA* gave them an answer: "My Teaching is not My Own, it comes from the One who sent

Me. 17 If anyone wants to do His Will, he will know whether My Teaching is from *ELOHIM* or I speak on My Own. 18 A person who speaks on his own is trying to win praise for himself; but a person who tries to win praise for the One who sent Him is Honest, there is nothing false about Him. 19 Did not Moses give you the *TORAH*? Yet not one of you obeys the *TORAH*! Why are you out to kill Me?" 20 "You have a *demon*!" the crowd answered. "Who is out to kill You?" 21 *YESHUA* answered them, "I did one thing; and because of this, all of you are amazed. 22 Moses gave you circumcision and not that it came from Moses but from the Patriarchs, and you do a sons circumcision on the Sabbath. 23 If a son is circumcised on the Sabbath so that the *TORAH* of Moses will not be broken, why are you angry with Me because I made a man's whole body well on the Sabbath? 24 Stop judging by surface appearances, and judge the right way!"

25 Some of the *Yerushalayim* people said, "Is not this the Man they are out to kill? 26 Yet here He is, speaking openly; and they do not say anything to Him. Could it be, that the authorities have actually concluded He is the MESSIAH? 27 But, we know where this Man comes from; but when the MESSIAH comes, no one will know where He comes from." 28 Whereupon *YESHUA*, continuing to teach in the TEMPLE

Courts, cried out, "Indeed you do know Me! And you know where I Am from! And I have not come on My Own! The One who sent Me is real. But Him you do not know! 29 I do know Him, because I Am with Him, and He sent Me!"

30 At this, they tried to arrest Him; but no one laid a hand on Him; because His time had not yet come. 31 However, many in the crowd put their faith in Him and said, "When the MESSIAH comes, will He do more miracles than this Man has done?"

32 The Pharisees heard the crowd whispering these things about *YESHUA*; so the head Priests and the Pharisees sent some of the TEMPLE Guards to arrest Him. 33 *YESHUA* said, "I will be with you only a little while longer; then I will go away to the One who sent Me. 34 You will look for Me and not find Me; indeed, where I Am, you cannot come." 35 The Jews said to themselves, "Where is this Man about to go, that we would not find Him? Does He intend to go to the Greek Diaspora and teach the Greek-speaking Jews? 36 And when He says, 'You will look for Me and not find Me; indeed, where I Am, you cannot come.'

37 Now on the last day of the festival of Tabernacle, the greatest day, *YESHUA* stood and cried out, "If anyone is

thirsty, let him keep coming to Me and drink! 38 Whoever puts his faith in Me, as the Scripture says, rivers of Living Waters will flow from his innermost being!" 39 (Now He said this about the SPIRIT, those whom put their faith in Him were to receive later, for the SPIRIT had not yet been given, because *YESHUA* had not yet been Glorified.)

40 On hearing His WORDS, some people in the crowd said, "Surely this Man is 'the PROPHET;'" 41 others said, "This is the MESSIAH." But others said, "How can the MESSIAH come from the Galilee? 42 Does not the *Tanakh* say that the MESSIAH is from **the seed of David,** II Samuel 7:12, and comes **from Bethlehem,** Micah 5:1 (2), the village where David lived?" 43 So the people were divided because of Him. 44 Some wanted to arrest Him, but no one laid a hand on Him.

45 The guards came back to the head Priests and the Pharisees, who asked them, "Why did you not bring Him in?" 46 The guards replied, "No one ever spoke the way this Man speaks!" 47 "You mean you have been taken in as well?" the Pharisees retorted. 48 "Has any of the authorities trusted Him? Or any of the Pharisees? No! 49 True, these people do, but they know nothing about the *TORAH*, they are under a curse!"

50 Nicodemus, the man who had gone to *YESHUA* before and

was one of them, said to them, 51 "Does our *TORAH* condemn a man before hearing from him and finding out what he is doing?" 52 They replied, "You are not from the Galilee too, are you? Study the *Tanakh*, and see for yourself that no prophet comes from the Galilee!" 53 Then they all left, each one to his own home.

8:1 But *YESHUA* went to the Mount of Olives. 2 At daybreak, He appeared again in the TEMPLE Court, where all the people gathered around Him, and He sat down to teach them. 3 The *TORAH*-Teachers and the Pharisees brought in a woman who had been caught committing adultery and made her stand in the center of the group. 4 Then they said to Him, "*RABBI*, this woman was caught in the very act of committing adultery. 5 Now in our *TORAH*, Moses commanded that such a woman be stoned to death. What do you say about it?" 6 They said this to trap Him, so that they might have ground for bringing charges against Him; but *YESHUA* bent down and began writing in the dust with His Finger. 7 When they kept questioning Him, He straightened up and said to them, "The one of you who is without sin, let him be the first to throw a stone at her." 8 Then He bent down and wrote in the dust again. 9 On hearing this, they began to leave, one by one, the older ones first, until He was left alone, with the woman still there. 10 Standing up, *YESHUA* said to her, "Where are they? Has no one condemned you?" 11 She said, "No one, sir." *YESHUA* said, "Neither do I condemn you. Now go, and do not sin anymore."

12 *YESHUA* spoke to them again: "I Am the Light of the world; whoever follows Me will never walk in darkness but will have the Light which gives Life." 13 So the Pharisees said to Him, "Now you are testifying on Your own behalf; Your Testimony is not valid." 14 *YESHUA* answered them, "Even if I do testify on My behalf, My Testimony is indeed valid; because I know where I come from and where I Am going; but you do not know where I came from or where I Am going. 15 You judge by merely human standards. As for Me, I pass Judgment on no one; 16 but if I were indeed to pass Judgment, My Judgment would be valid; because it is not I alone who judge, but I and the One who sent Me. 17 And even in your *Torah* it is written that the testimony of two people is valid. 18 I Myself testify on My Own behalf, and so does the FATHER who sent Me."

19 They said to Him, "Where is this 'FATHER' of Yours?" *YESHUA* answered, "You know neither Me nor My FATHER; if you knew Me, you would know My FATHER too." 20 He said these things when He was teaching in the TEMPLE

Treasury Room; yet no one arrested Him, because His time had not yet come.

21 Again *YESHUA* told them, "I Am going away, and you will look for Me and you will die in your sin. Where I Am going, you cannot come." 22 The Jews said, "Is He going to commit suicide? Is that what He means when He says, 'Where I Am going, you cannot come'?" 23 *YESHUA* said to them, "You are from below, I Am from above; you are of this world, I Am not of this world. 24 This is why I said to you that you will die in your sins; for if you do not have faith that I Am [who I say I Am], you will die in your sins."

25 At this, they said to Him, "You? Who are you?" *YESHUA* answered, "Just what I have been telling you from the start. 26 There are many things I could say about you, and many judgments I could make. However, the One who sent Me is True; so I say in the world only what I have heard from Him." 27 They did not understand that He was talking to them about the FATHER. 28 So *YESHUA* said, "When you lift up the SON of Man, then you will know that I Am [who I say I Am], and that of Myself I do nothing, but say only what the FATHER has taught Me. 29 Also, the One who sent me is still with Me; He did not leave Me to Myself, because I always do what pleases Him."

30 Many people who heard Him say these things put their faith in Him. 31 So *YESHUA* said to the Jews who had put their faith in Him, "If you obey what I say, then you are really My Disciples, 32 you will know the Truth, and the Truth will set you Free." 33 They answered, "We are the seed of Abraham and have never been slaves to anyone; so what do You mean by saying, 'You will be set Free'?" 34 *YESHUA* answered them, "Yes, indeed! I tell you that everyone who practices sin is a slave of sin. 35 Now a slave does not remain with a family forever, but a son does remain with it forever. 36 So if the SON Frees you, you will really be Free! 37 I know you are the seed of Abraham. Yet you are out to kill Me, because what I Am saying makes no headway in you. 38 I say what My FATHER has shown Me; you do what your father has told you!"

39 They answered him, "Our father is Abraham." *YESHUA* replied, "If you are children of Abraham, then do the things Abraham did! 40 As it is, you are out to kill Me, a Man who has told you the truth which I heard from *ELOHIM*. Abraham did nothing like that! 41 You are doing the things your father does." "We are not illegitimate children!" They said to him. "We have only one FATHER, *ELOHIM*!" 42 *YESHUA* replied to them, "If *ELOHIM* were your FATHER, you would love Me; because I came out from *ELOHIM*; and now I have arrived

here. I did not come on My own; He sent Me. 43 Why do you not understand what I Am saying? Because you cannot bear to listen to My Message. 44 You belong to your father, Satan, and you want to carry out your father's desires. From the start he was a murderer, and he has never stood by the Truth, because there is no Truth in him. When he tells a lie, he is speaking in character; because he is a liar; indeed, the inventor of the lie! 45 But as for Me, because I tell the Truth you do not believe Me. 46 Which one of you can show Me where I Am wrong? If I Am telling the Truth, why do you not believe Me? 47 Whoever belongs to *ELOHIM* listens to what *ELOHIM* says; the reason you do not listen is that you do not belong to *ELOHIM*."

48 The Jews answered Him, "Are we not right in saying You are from Samaria and have a *demon*?" 49 *YESHUA* replied, "Me? I have no *demon*. I Am honoring My FATHER. But you dishonor Me. 50 I Am not seeking praise for Myself. There is One who is seeking it, and He is the Judge. 51 Yes, indeed! I tell you that whoever obeys My Teaching will never see death."

52 The Jews said to Him, "Now we know for sure that You have a *demon*! Abraham died, and so did the prophets; yet You say, 'Whoever obeys My Teaching will never taste death.' 53

Abraham our father died; you are not greater than He, are You? And the prophets also died. Who do You think You are?" 54 *YESHUA* answered, "If I praise Myself, My praise counts for nothing. The One who is praising Me is My FATHER, the very One about whom you keep saying, 'He is our *ELOHIM.*' 55 Now you have not known Him, but I do know Him; indeed, if I were to say that I do not know Him, I would be a liar like you! But I do know Him, and I obey His WORD. 56 Abraham, your father, was glad that he would see My Day; then he saw it and was overjoyed."

57 "Why, you are not yet fifty years old," the Jews replied, "And you have seen Abraham?" 58 *YESHUA* said to them, "Yes, indeed! Before Abraham came into being, I AM!" 59 At this, they picked up stones to throw at Him; but *YESHUA* was hidden and left the TEMPLE Grounds.

9:1 As *YESHUA* passed along, He saw a man blind from birth. 2 His Disciples asked Him, "*RABBI*, who sinned, this man or his parents, to cause him to be born blind?" 3 *YESHUA* answered, "His blindness is due neither to his sin nor to that of his parents; it happened so that *ELOHIM'S* Power might be seen at work in him. 4 As long as it is day, we must keep doing the work of the One who sent Me; the night is coming, when no one can work. 5 While I Am in the world, I Am the Light of the World."

6 Having said this, He spit on the ground, made some mud with the saliva, put the mud on the man's eyes, 7 and said to him, "Go, wash off in the Pool of Siloam!" (The name means "sent.") So he went and washed and came away seeing.

8 His neighbors and those who previously had seen him begging said, "Is not this the man who used to sit and beg?" 9 Some said, "Yes, he is the one;" while others said, "No, but he looks like him." However, he himself said, "I am the one." 10 "How were your eyes opened?" They asked him. 11 He answered, "The Man called *YESHUA* made mud, put it on my eyes, and told me, 'Go to Siloam and wash!' So I went; and as soon as I had washed, I could see." 12 They said to him, "Where is He?" and he replied, "I do not know."

13 They took the man who had been blind to the Pharisees. 14 Now the day on which *YESHUA* had made the mud and opened his eyes was the Sabbath. 15 So the Pharisees asked him again how he had become able to see; and he told them, "He put mud on my eyes, then I washed, and now I can see." 16 At this, some of the Pharisees said, "This Man is not from *ELOHIM*,

because He does not keep the Sabbath." But others said, "How could a man who is a sinner do miracles like these?" And there was a split among them. 17 So once more they spoke to the blind man: "Since you are the one whose eyes He opened, what do you say about Him?" He replied: "He is a Prophet."

18 The Jews, however, were unwilling to believe that he had formerly been blind, but now could see, until they had summoned the man's parents. 19 They asked them, "Is this your son who you say was born blind? How is it that now he can see?" 20 His parents answered, "We know that this is our son and that he was born blind; 21 but how it is that he can see now, we do not know; or do we know who opened his eyes. Ask him, he is old enough, he can speak for himself!" 22 The parents said this because they were afraid of the Jews, for the Jews had already agreed that anyone who acknowledged *YESHUA* as the MESSIAH would be banned from the Assembly. 23 This is why his parents said, "he is old enough, ask him."

24 So a second time they called the man who had been blind; and they said to him, "Swear to *ELOHIM* that you will tell the truth! We know that this Man is a sinner." 25 He answered, "Whether He is a sinner or not I do not know. One thing I do know: I was blind, now I see." 26 So they said to him, "What

did He do to you? How did He open your eyes?" 27 "I already told you," he answered, "And you did not listen. Why do you want to hear it again? Maybe you too want to become His Disciples?" 28 Then they railed at him. "You may be His Disciple," they said, "But we are disciples of Moses! 29 We know that *ELOHIM* has spoken to Moses, but this one, we do not know where He is from!" 30 "What a strange thing," the man answered, "That you do not know where He is from and considering that He opened my eyes! 31 We know that *ELOHIM* does not listen to sinners; but if anyone fears *ELOHIM* and does His Will, *ELOHIM* does listen to him. 32 In all history no one has ever heard of someone opening the eyes of a man born blind. 33 If this Man were not from *ELOHIM*, He could not do a thing!" 34 "Why, you sinner!" They retorted, "Are you lecturing us?" And they threw him out.

35 *YESHUA* heard that they had thrown the man out. He found him and said, "Do you have faith in the SON of Man?" 36 "Sir," he answered, "Tell me who He is, so that I can have faith in Him." 37 *YESHUA* said to him, "You have seen Him. In fact, He is the One speaking with you now." 38 "LORD, I have faith!" He said, and he kneeled down in front of Him.

39 *YESHUA* said, "It is to Judge that I came into this world, so that those who do not see might see, and those who do see

might become blind." 40 Some of the Pharisees nearby heard this and said to Him, "So we are blind too, are we?" 41 *YESHUA* answered them, "If you were blind, you would not be guilty of sin. But since you still say, 'We see,' your guilt remains.

5:1 After this, was one of *YAHVEH'S Appointed Times* and *YESHUA* went up to *Yerushalayim*. 2 In *Yerushalayim*, by the Sheep Gate, is a pool called in Aramaic, Bethzatha, 3 in which lay a crowd of invalids: blind and lame and crippled. 4* 5 One man was there who had been ill for thirty-eight years. 6 *YESHUA*, seeing this man and knowing that he had been there a long time, said to him, "Do you want to be healed?" 7 The sick man answered, "I have no one to put me in the pool when the Water is disturbed; and while I am trying to get there, someone goes ahead of me." 8 *YESHUA* said to him, "Get up, pick up your mat and walk!" 9 Immediately the man was healed, and he picked up his mat and walked. Now that day was the Sabbath, 10 so the Jews said to the man who had been healed, "It is the Sabbath! It's against the *TORAH* for you to carry your mat!" 11 But he answered them, "The Man who healed me, He is the One who told me, 'Pick up your mat and walk.'" 12 They asked him, "Who is the Man who told you to pick it up and walk?" 13 But the man who had been healed did not know who It was, because *YESHUA* had slipped away into the crowd.

4* Some manuscripts have verses 3b-4...waiting for the Water to move; 4 for at certain times an angel of *ADONAI* went down into the pool and disturbed the Water, and whoever stepped into the Water first after it was disturbed was healed of whatever disease he had.

14 Afterwards *YESHUA* found him in the TEMPLE Court and said to him, "See, you are well! Now stop sinning, or something worse may happen to you!" 15 The man went off and told the Jews it was *YESHUA* who had healed him; 16 and on account of this, the Jews began harassing *YESHUA* because He did these things on the Sabbath. 17 But He answered them, "My FATHER has been working until now, and I, too, am working." 18 This answer made the Jews all the more intent on killing Him; not only was He breaking the Sabbath; but also, by saying that *ELOHIM* was His Own FATHER, He was claiming equality with *ELOHIM*. 19 Therefore, *YESHUA* said to them: "Yes, indeed! I tell you that the SON cannot do anything on His own, but only what He sees the FATHER doing; whatever the FATHER does, the SON does, too.

20 For the FATHER loves the SON and shows Him everything He does; and will show Him even greater things than these, so that you will be amazed. 21 Just as the FATHER raises the dead and makes them alive, so too the SON makes alive anyone He wants. 22 The FATHER does not Judge anyone but has entrusted all Judgment to the SON, 23 so that all may honor the SON as they honor the FATHER. Whoever fails to honor the SON is not honoring the FATHER who sent Him. 24 Yes, indeed! I tell you that whoever hears what I Am saying and has faith in the One who sent Me has Eternal Life; that is, he will not come up for Judgment but has already crossed over from death to Life! 25 Yes, indeed I tell you that there is coming a time; in fact, it is already here; when the dead will hear the Voice of the SON of *ELOHIM*, and those who listen will come to Life. 26 For just as the FATHER has Life in Himself, so He has given the SON Life to have Himself. 27 Also He has given Him Authority to execute Judgment, because He is the SON of Man. 28 Do not be surprised at this; because the time is coming when all who are in the grave will hear His Voice 29 and come out; those who have done good to a Resurrection of Life, and those who have done evil to a Resurrection of Judgment. 30 I cannot do a thing on My Own. As I hear, I Judge; and My Judgment is right; because I do not

seek My Own desire, but the desire of the One who sent Me.

31 "If I testify on My Own behalf, My Testimony is not valid. 32 But there is someone else testifying on My behalf, and I know that the Testimony He is making is valid; 33 you have sent to John, and he has testified to the Truth. 34 Not that I collect human testimony; rather, I say these things so that you might be saved. 35 He was a lamp burning and shining, and for a little while you were willing to bask in his light.

36 "But I have a Testimony that is greater than John's. For the things the FATHER has given Me to do, the very things I Am doing now, testify on My behalf that the FATHER has sent Me.

37 "In addition, the FATHER who sent Me has Himself Testified on My behalf. But you have never heard His Voice or seen His Shape; 38 moreover, His WORD does not stay in you, because you do not have faith in the One He sent. 39 You keep examining the *Tanakh* because you think that in it you have Eternal Life. Those very Scriptures bear witness to Me, 40 but you would not come to Me in order to have Life!

41 "I do not collect praise from men, 42 but I do know you people; I know that you have no love for *ELOHIM* in you! 43 I have come in My FATHER'S NAME, and you do not accept

Me; if someone else comes in his own name, him you will accept. 44 How can you have faith? You are busy collecting praise from each other, instead of seeking praise from *ELOHIM* only.

45 "But do not think that it is I who will be your accuser before the FATHER. Do you know who will accuse you? Moses, the very one you have counted on! 46 For if you really believed Moses, you would believe Me; because it was about Me that he wrote. 47 But if you do not believe what he wrote, how are you going to believe what I say?"

10:1 "Yes, indeed! I tell you, the person who does not enter the sheep-pen through the door, but climbs in some other way, is a thief and a robber. 2 But the One who goes in through the gate is the sheep's own Shepherd. 3 This is the One the gate-keeper admits, and the sheep hear His Voice. He calls His Own Sheep, each one by name, and leads them out. 4 After taking out all that are His Own, He goes on ahead of them; and the sheep follow Him because they recognize His Voice. 5 They never follow a stranger but will run away from him, because strangers' voices are unfamiliar to them."

6 *YESHUA* used this indirect manner of speaking with them,

but they did not understand what He was talking to them about. 7 So *YESHUA* said to them again, "yes, indeed! I tell you that I Am the Gate for the sheep. 8 All those who have come before Me have been thieves and robbers, but the sheep did not listen to them. 9 I Am the Gate; if someone enters through Me, he will be safe and will go in and out and find pasture. 10 The thief comes only in order to steal, kill and destroy; I have come so that they may have Life, Life in its fullest measure.

11 "I Am the Good Shepherd. The Good Shepherd lays down His Life for the sheep. 12 The hired hand, since he is not a shepherd and the sheep are not his own, sees the wolf coming, abandons the sheep and runs away. Then the wolf drags them off and scatters them. 13 The hired worker behaves like this because that is all he is, a hired worker; so it does not matter to him what happens to the sheep. 14 I Am the Good Shepherd; I know My Own, and My Own know Me; 15 just as the FATHER knows Me, and I know the FATHER; and I lay down My Life on behalf of the sheep. 16 Also I have other sheep which are not from this pen; I need to bring them, and they will hear My Voice; and there will be One Flock, One Shepherd.

17 "This is why the FATHER loves Me: because I lay down My Life; in order to take it up again! 18 No one takes it away from Me; on the contrary, I lay it down of My Own free will. I

have the Power to lay it down, and I have the Power to take it up again. This is what My FATHER Commanded Me to do."

19 Again there was a split among the Jews because of what He said. 20 Many of them said, "He has a *demon!*" and "He is crazy! Why do you listen to him?" 21 Others said, "These are not the deeds of a man who is *demonized*. How can a *demon* open blind people's eyes?"

22 Then came *Chanukkah* in *Yerushalayim*. It was winter, 23 and *YESHUA* was walking around inside the TEMPLE area, in Solomon's Porch. 24 So the Jews surrounded Him and said to Him, "How much longer are you going to keep us in suspense? If you are the MESSIAH, tell us publicly!" 25 *YESHUA* answered them, "I have already told you, and you do not have faith in Me. The works I do in My FATHER'S NAME testify on my behalf, 26 but the reason you do not have faith is that you are not included among My Sheep. 27 My Sheep listen to My Voice, I recognize them, they follow Me, 28 and I give them Eternal Life. They will absolutely never be destroyed, and no one will snatch them from My Hands. 29 My FATHER, who gave them to Me, is greater than all; and no one can snatch them from the FATHER'S Hands. 30 I and the FATHER are One."

31 Once again the Jews picked up rocks in order to stone Him. 32 *YESHUA* answered them, "You have seen Me do many good deeds that reflect the FATHER'S Power; for which one of these deeds are you stoning Me?" 33 The Jews replied, "We are not stoning you for any good deed, but for blasphemy; because You, who are only a man, are making Yourself out to be *ELOHIM*." 34 *YESHUA* answered them, "Is it not written in your *Torah*, Psalms 82:6 **'I have said, "You people are elohim'?"** 35 If He called *'elohim'* the people to whom the WORD of *ELOHIM* was addressed (and the *Tanakh* cannot be broken), 36 then are you telling the One whom the FATHER set apart as HOLY and sent into the world, 'You are committing blasphemy,' just because I said, 'I Am a SON of *ELOHIM*'?

37 If I Am not doing the deeds that reflect My FATHER'S Power, do not have faith in Me. 38 But if I Am, then even if you do not have faith in Me, have faith in the deeds; so that you may understand once and for all that the FATHER is united with Me, and I Am united with the FATHER." 39 One more time they tried to arrest Him, but He slipped out of their hands.

40 He went off again beyond the Jordan, where John had been witnessing *immersions* at first, and stayed there. 41 Many

people came to Him and said, "John performed no miracles, but everything John said about this Man was true." 42 And many people there put their faith in Him

3:22 After this, *YESHUA* and His Disciples went out into the countryside of Judea, where He stayed awhile with them witnessing people *immersing.* 23 John too was witnessing *immersions* at the spring of Aenon, near Salem, because there was plenty of water there; and people kept coming to *immerse.* 24 (This was before John's imprisonment.)

25 A discussion arose between some of John's disciples and a Jew about ceremonial washing; 26 and they came to John and said to him, "*Rabbi*, you know the Man who was with you on the other side of the Jordan, the One you spoke about? Well, here He is, witnessing *immersions* and everyone is going to Him!" 27 John answered, "No one can receive anything unless it has been given to him from Heaven. 28 You yourselves can confirm that I did not say I was the MESSIAH, but that I have been sent ahead of Him. 29 The Bridegroom is the One who has the Bride; but the Bridegroom's Friend, who stands and listens to Him, is overjoyed at the sound of the Bridegroom's Voice. So this joy of mine is now complete. 30 He must

become more important, while I become less important.

31 "He who comes from above is above all. He who is from the earth is from the earth and talks from an earthly point of view; He who comes from Heaven is above all. 32 He testifies about what He has actually seen and heard, yet no one accepts what He says! 33 Whoever does accept what He says puts his seal on the fact that *ELOHIM* is True, 34 because the One whom *ELOHIM* sent speaks *ELOHIM'S* WORDS. For *ELOHIM* does not give Him the SPIRIT in limited degree. 35 The FATHER loves the SON and has put everything in His Hands. 36 Whoever has faith in the SON has Eternal Life. But whoever disobeys the SON will not see that Life but remains subject to *ELOHIM'S* Wrath."

4:1 When *YESHUA* learned that the Pharisees had heard He was making more Disciples and witnessing more *immersions* than John 2 (although it was not *YESHUA* Himself who was witnessing *immersions* but His Disciples), 3 *YESHUA* left Judea and set out again for the Galilee. 4 This meant that He had to pass through Samaria.

5 He came to a town in Samaria called Shechem, near the field Jacob had given to his son Joseph. 6 Jacob's well was there; so *YESHUA*, exhausted from His travel, sat down by the well; it

was about noon. 7 A woman from Samaria came to draw some water; and *YESHUA* said to her, "Give Me a drink of water." 8 (His Disciples had gone into town to buy food.) 9 The woman from Samaria said to Him, "How is it that You, a Jew, ask for water from me, a woman of Samaria?" (For Jews do not associate with people from Samaria.) 10 *YESHUA* answered her, "If you knew *ELOHIM'S* Gift, that is, who it is saying to you, 'Give Me a drink of water,' then you would have asked Him; and He would have given you Living Waters."

11 She said to Him, "Sir, you do not have a bucket, and the well is deep; so where do you get this 'Living Water?' 12 You are not greater than our father Jacob, are You? He gave us this well and drank from it, and so did his sons and his cattle." 13 *YESHUA* answered, "Everyone who drinks this water will get thirsty again, 14 but whoever drinks the Water I will give him will never be thirsty again! On the contrary, the Water I give him will become a Spring of Water inside him, welling up into Eternal Life!"

15 "Sir, give me this Water" the woman said to Him, "So that I would not have to be thirsty and keep coming here to draw water." 16 He said to her, "Go, call your husband, and come back." 17 She answered, "I do not have a husband." *YESHUA* said to her, "You are right, you do not have a husband! 18 You

have had five husbands in the past, and you are not married to the man you are living with now! You have spoken the truth!"

19 "Sir, I can see that You are a Prophet," the woman replied. 20 "Our fathers worshipped on this mountain, but you people say that the place where one has to worship is in *Yerushalayim*." 21 *YESHUA* said, "Lady, believe me, the time is coming when you will worship the FATHER neither on this mountain nor in *Yerushalayim*. 22 You people do not know what you are worshipping; we worship what we do know, because salvation comes from the Jews. 23 But the time is coming and indeed, it is here now; when the true worshippers will worship the FATHER spiritually and truly, for these are the kind of people the FATHER wants worshipping Him. 24 *ELOHIM* is SPIRIT; and worshippers must worship Him spiritually and truly."

25 The woman replied, "I know that *MASHIACH* is coming" (that is, "The one who has been anointed"). "When He comes, He will tell us everything." 26 *YESHUA* said to her, "I, the person speaking to you, Am He."

27 Just then, His Disciples arrived. They were amazed that He was talking with a woman; but none of them said, "What do you want?" or, "Why are You talking with her?" 28 So the

woman left her water-jar, went back to the town and said to the people there, 29 "Come, see a Man who told me everything I have ever done. Could it be that this is the MESSIAH?" 30 They left the town and began coming toward Him.

31 Meanwhile, the disciples were urging *YESHUA*, "*RABBI*, eat something." 32 But He answered, "I have food to eat that you do not know about." 33 At this, the disciples asked one another, "Could someone have brought Him food?" 34 *YESHUA* said to them, "My food is to do what the One who sent Me wants and to bring His Work to completion. 35 Do you not have a saying, 'Four more months and then the harvest'? Well, what I say to you is: open your eyes and look at the fields! They are already ripe for harvest! 36 The one who reaps receives his wages and gathers fruit for Eternal Life, so that the reaper and the sower may be glad together; 37 for in this matter, the proverb, 'One sows and another reaps,' holds true. 38 I sent you to reap what you have not worked for. Others have done the hard labor, and you have benefited from their work."

39 Many people from that town in Samaria put their faith in Him because of the woman's testimony, "He told me all the things I did." 40 So when these people from Samaria came to Him, they asked Him to stay with them. He stayed two days,

41 and many more came to faith because of what He said. 42 They said to the woman, "We no longer have faith because of what you said, because we have heard for ourselves. We know indeed that this Man really is the Savior of the World."

43 After the two days, He went on from there toward the Galilee. 44 Now *YESHUA* Himself said, "A Prophet is not respected in His Own country." 45 But when He arrived in the Galilee, the people there welcomed Him, because they had seen all He had done at the festival in *Yerushalayim*; since they had been there too.

46 He went again to Cana in the Galilee, where He had turned the water into wine. An officer in the Royal Service was there; his son was ill in Capernaum. 47 This man, on hearing that *YESHUA* had come from Judea to the Galilee, went and asked Him to come down and heal his son, for he was at the point of death. 48 *YESHUA* answered, "Unless you people see signs and miracles, you simply will not have faith!" 49 The officer said to Him, "Sir, come down before my child dies." 50 *YESHUA* replied, "You may go, your son is alive." The man believed what *YESHUA* said and left. 51 As he was going down, his servants met him with the news that his son was alive 52 So he asked them at what time he had gotten better; and they said, "The fever left him yesterday at one o'clock in

the afternoon." 53 The father knew that it was the very hour when *YESHUA* had told him, "Your son is alive;" and he and all his household had faith. 54 This was a second sign that *YESHUA* did; He did it after He had come from Judea into the Galilee.

11:1 There was a man who had fallen sick. His name was Lazarus, and he came from Bethany, the village where Mary and her sister Martha lived. 2 (This Mary, whose brother Lazarus had become sick, is the one who poured perfume on the LORD and wiped His Feet with her hair.) 3 So the sisters sent a message to *YESHUA*, "LORD, the man you love is sick." 4 On hearing it, He said, "This sickness will not end in death. No, it is for *ELOHIM'S* Glory, so that the SON of *ELOHIM* may receive Glory through it."

5 *YESHUA* loved Martha and her sister and Lazarus; 6 so when He heard he was sick, first He stayed where He was two more days; 7 then, after this, He said to the disciples, "Let us go back to Judea." 8 The disciples replied, "*RABBI*! Just a short while ago the Jews were out to stone You; and You want to go back there?" 9 *YESHUA* answered, "Are not there twelve hours of daylight? If a person walks during daylight, he does not

stumble; because he sees the Light of this World. 10 But if a person walks at night, he does stumble; because he has no Light with him."

11 *YESHUA* said these things, and afterwards He said to the disciples, "Our friend Lazarus has gone to sleep; but I Am going in order to wake him up." 12 The disciples said to Him, "LORD, if he has gone to sleep, he will get better." 13 Now *YESHUA* had used the phrase to speak about Lazarus's death, but they thought He had been talking literally about sleep. 14 So *YESHUA* told them in plain language, "Lazarus has died. 15 And for your sakes, I Am glad that I was not there, so that you may come to have faith. But let us go to him." 16 Then Thomas (the name means "Twin") said to his fellow disciples, "Yes, we should go, so that we can die with Him!"

17 On arrival, *YESHUA* found that Lazarus had already been in the tomb for four days. 18 Now Bethany was about two miles from *Yerushalayim*, 19 and many of the Jews had come to Martha and Mary in order to comfort them at the loss of their brother. 20 So when Martha heard that *YESHUA* was coming, she went out to meet Him; but Mary continued sitting *shiv'ah* in the house.

21 Martha said to *YESHUA*, "LORD, if you had been here, my

brother would not have died. 22 Even now I know that whatever you ask of *ELOHIM*, *ELOHIM* will give You." 23 *YESHUA* said to her, "Your brother will rise again." 24 Martha said, "I know that he will rise again at the Resurrection on the Last Day." 25 *YESHUA* said to her, "I Am the Resurrection and the Life! Whoever puts his faith in Me will live, even if he dies; 26 and everyone living and having faith in Me will never die. Do you believe this?" 27 She said to Him, "Yes, LORD, I believe that you are the MESSIAH, the SON of *ELOHIM*, the One coming into the world."

28 After saying this, she went off and secretly called Mary, her sister: "The *RABBI* is here and is calling for you." 29 When she heard this, she jumped up and went to Him. 30 *YESHUA* had not yet come into the village but was still where Martha had met Him; 31 so when the Jews who had been with Mary in the house comforting her saw her get up quickly and go out, they followed her, thinking she was going to the tomb to mourn there.

32 When Mary came to where *YESHUA* was and saw Him, she fell at His Feet and said to Him, "LORD, if You had been here, my brother would not have died." 33 When *YESHUA* saw her crying, and also the Jews who came with her crying, He was deeply moved and also troubled. 34 He said, "Where have you

buried him?" They said, "LORD, come and see." 35 *YESHUA* cried; 36 so the Jews there said, "See how He loved him!" 37 But some of them said, "He opened the blind man's eyes. Could He not have kept this one from dying?"

38 *YESHUA*, again deeply moved, came to the tomb. It was a cave, and a stone was lying in front of the entrance. 39 *YESHUA* said, "Take the stone away!" Martha, the sister of the dead man, said to *YESHUA*, "By now his body must smell, for it has been four days since he died!" 40 *YESHUA* said to her, "Did I not tell you that if you, having faith, you will see the Glory of *ELOHIM*?" 41 So they removed the stone. *YESHUA* looked upward and said, "FATHER, I thank You that You have heard Me. 42 I Myself know that You always hear Me, but I say this because of the crowd standing around, so that they may believe that You have sent Me." 43 Having said this, He shouted, "Lazarus! Come out!" 44 The man who had been dead came out, his hands and feet wrapped in strips of linen and his face covered with a cloth. *YESHUA* said to them, "Unwrap him, and let him go!" 45 At this, many of the Jews who had come to visit Mary, and had seen what *YESHUA* had done, had faith in Him.

46 But some of them went off to the Pharisees and told them what He had done. 47 So the head Priests and the Pharisees

called a meeting of the *Sanhedrin* and said, "What are we going to do? For this Man is performing many miracles. 48 If we let Him keep going on this way, everyone will have faith in Him, and the Romans will come and destroy both the TEMPLE and the nation." 49 But one of them, Caiaphas, who was The High Priest that year, said to them, "You people do not know anything! 50 You do not see that it is better for you if one man dies on behalf of the people, so that the whole nation would not be destroyed." 51 Now he did not speak this way on his own initiative; rather, since he was The High Priest that year, he was prophesying that *YESHUA* was about to die on behalf of the nation, 52 and not for the nation alone, but so that He might gather into one the scattered Children of *ELOHIM*.

53 From that day on, they made plans to have Him put to death. 54 Therefore *YESHUA* no longer walked around openly among the Jews but went away from there into the region near the wilderness, to a town called Ephraim, and stayed there with His Disciples.

6:1 Sometime later, *YESHUA* went over to the far side of Sea of Galilee, 2 and a large crowd followed Him, because they had seen the miracles He had performed on the sick. 3

YESHUA went up into the hills and sat down there with His Disciples. 4 Now *YAHVEH'S Appointed Time* of Passover was coming up; 5 so when *YESHUA* looked up and saw that a large crowd was approaching, He said to Philip, "Where will we be able to buy bread, so that these people can eat?" 6 (Now *YESHUA* said this to test Philip, for *YESHUA* Himself knew what He was about to do.) 7 Philip answered, "Half a year's wages would not buy enough bread for them, each one would get only a bite!" 8 One of the disciples, Andrew the brother of Simon Peter, said to Him, 9 "There is a young fellow here who has five loaves of barley bread and two fish. But how far will they go among so many?"

10 *YESHUA* said, "Have the people sit down." There was a lot of grass there, so they sat down. The number of men was about five thousand. 11 Then *YESHUA* took the loaves of bread, and, after saying a Blessing, *(Baruch atah ADONAI ELO-HAI-NU MELEK ha'olam ha-motzi lechem min ha-arets.* AH-MAYN. Blessed are You, *ADONAI*, our *ELOHIM*, Ruler of the universe, who brings bread from out of the earth.) gave to all who were sitting there, and likewise with the fish, as much as they wanted. 2 After they had eaten their fill, He told His Disciples, "Gather the leftover pieces, so that nothing gets wasted." 13 They gathered them and filled twelve baskets with

the pieces from the five barley loaves left by those who had eaten.

[Witnesses: Matthew 14:13-21 "On hearing about this, YESHUA left in a boat to be by Himself in the wilderness. But the people learned of it and followed Him from the towns by land. 14 So when He came ashore, He saw a huge crowd; and, filled with compassion for them, He healed those of them who were sick. 15 As evening approached, the disciples came to Him and said, 'This is a remote place and it is getting late. Send the crowds away, so that they can go and buy food for themselves in the villages.' 16 But YESHUA replied, 'They do not need to go away. Give them something to eat, yourselves!' 17 'All we have with us,' they said 'Is five loaves of bread and two fish.' 18 He said, 'Bring them here to Me.' 19 After instructing the crowds to sit down on the grass, He took the five loaves and the two fish and, looking up to Heaven, said a Blessing. Then He broke the loaves and gave them to the disciples, who gave them to the crowds. 20 They all ate as much as they wanted, and they took up twelve baskets full of pieces left over. 21 Those eating numbered about five thousand men, plus women and children. Mark 6:34-44 and Luke 9:11-

17 repeat Matthew.]

6:14 When the people saw the miracle He had performed, they said, "This has to be 'the PROPHET' who is supposed to come into the world." 15 *YESHUA* knew that they were on the point of coming and seizing Him, in order to make Him King so He went back to the hills again. This time He went by Himself.

16 When evening came, His Disciples went down to the lake, 17 got into a boat and set out across the lake toward Capernaum. By now it was dark, *YESHUA* had not yet joined them, 18 and the sea was getting rough, because a strong wind was blowing. 19 They had rowed three or four miles when they saw *YESHUA* approaching the boat, walking on the lake! They were terrified; 20 but He said to them, "Stop being afraid, it is I." 21 Then they were willing to take Him into the boat, and instantly the boat reached the land they were heading for.

[Witnesses: Matthew 14:22-34 "Immediately He had the disciples get in the boat and go on ahead of Him to the other side, while He sent the crowds away. 23 After He had sent the crowds away, He went up into the hills by Himself to pray.

Night came on, and He was there alone. 24 But by this time, the boat was several miles from shore, battling a rough sea and a headwind. 25 Around four o'clock in the morning, He came toward them, walking on the lake! 26 When the disciples saw Him walking on the lake, they were terrified. 'It is a ghost!' They said and screamed with fear. 27 But at once *YESHUA* spoke to them. 'Courage,' He said, 'it is I. Stop being afraid.' 28 Then Peter called to Him, 'LORD, if it is really You, tell me to come to You on the water.' 29 'Come!' He said. So Peter got out of the boat and walked on the water toward *YESHUA*. 30 But when he saw the wind, he became afraid; and as he began to sink, he yelled, 'LORD! Save me!' 31 *YESHUA* immediately stretched out His hand, took hold of him, and said to him, 'Such little faith! Why did you doubt?' 32 As they went up into the boat, the wind ceased. 33 The men in the boat fell down before Him and exclaimed, 'You really are *ELOHIM'S SON!*' Having made the crossing, they landed at Gennesaret." Mark 6:45-53 repeats Matthew.]

6:22 The next day, the crowd which had stayed on the other side of the lake noticed that there had been only one boat there, and that *YESHUA* had not entered the boat with His Disciples, but that the disciples had been alone when they sailed off. 23 Then other boats, from Tiberias, came ashore near the place where they had eaten the bread after the LORD had made the Blessing. 24 Accordingly, when the crowd saw that neither YESHUA nor His Disciples were there, they themselves boarded the boats and made for Capernaum in search of YESHUA.

25 When they found Him on the other side of the lake, they asked Him, "*RABBI*, when did you get here?" 26 YESHUA answered, "Yes, indeed! I tell you, you are not looking for Me because you saw miraculous signs, but because you ate the bread and had all you wanted! 27 Do not work for the food which passes away but for the food that stays on into Eternal Life, which the SON of Man will give you. For this is the One on whom *ELOHIM* the FATHER has put His Seal."

28 So they said to Him, "what should we do in order to perform the Works of *ELOHIM*?" 29 YESHUA answered, "Here is what the Work of *ELOHIM* is: to have faith in the One He sent!"

30 They said to Him, well, what miracle will You do for us, so that we may see it and have faith in You? What work can You perform? 31 Our fathers ate manna in the wilderness; as it says

in the *Tanakh*, Psalms 78:24 and Nehemiah 9:15 '**He gave them Bread from Heaven** to eat.' 32 *YESHUA* said to them, "Yes, indeed! I tell you it was not Moses who gave the Bread from Heaven; 33 for *ELOHIM'S* Bread is the One who comes down out of Heaven and gives Life to the world."

34 They said to Him, "Sir, give us this Bread from now on." 35 *YESHUA* answered, "I Am the Bread which is Life! Whoever comes to Me will never go hungry, and whoever has faith in Me will never be thirsty. 36 I told you that you have seen but still do not have faith. 37 Everyone the FATHER gives Me will come to Me, and whoever comes to Me I will certainly not turn away. 38 For I have come down from Heaven not to do My Own Will but the Will of the One who sent Me. 39 And this is the will of the One who sent Me: that I should not lose any of all those He has given Me, but, should raise them up on the Last Day. 40 Yes, this is the Will of My FATHER: that all who see the SON and have faith in Him should have Eternal Life, and that I should raise him up on the Last Days."

41 At this the Jews began grumbling about Him because He said, "I Am the Bread which has come down from Heaven." 42 They said, "Is not this *YESHUA* SON of Joseph? We know His Father and Mother! How can He now say, I have come down from Heaven?'" 43 *YESHUA* answered them, "Stop grumbling

to each other! 44. No one can come to Me unless the FATHER; the One who sent Me; draws him. And I will raise him up on the Last Days. 45 It is written in the Prophets, Isaiah 54:13 **'They will all be taught by *ADONAI*.'** Everyone who listens to the FATHER and learns from Him comes to Me. 46 Not that anyone has seen the FATHER except the One who is from *ELOHIM*, He has seen the FATHER. 47 Yes, indeed! I tell you, whoever has faith has Eternal Life: 48 I Am the Bread which is Life. 49 Your fathers ate manna in the wilderness; they died. 50. But the Bread that has comes down from Heaven is such that a person may eat It and not die. 51 I Am the Living Bread that has come down from Heaven; if anyone eats this Bread, he will live forever. Furthermore, the Bread that I will give is My Own Flesh; and I will give it for the Life of the world." 52 At this, the Jews disputed with one another, saying, "How can this Man give us His Flesh to eat?" 53 Then *YESHUA* said to them, "Yes, indeed! I tell you that unless you eat the Flesh of the SON of Man and drink His Blood, you do not have life in yourselves. 54 Whoever eats My Flesh and drinks My Blood has Eternal Life; that is, I will raise him up in the Last Days. 55 For My Flesh is True Food, and My Blood is True Drink. 56 Whoever eats My Flesh and drinks My Blood lives in Me, and I live in him. 57 Just as the living FATHER sent Me, and I live through the FATHER, so also whoever eats Me will live through Me. 58 So this is the Bread that has come down from Heaven; it is not like the bread the fathers ate; they are dead, but whoever eats this Bread will Live Forever!" 59 He said these things as He was teaching in an Assembly in Capernaum.

60 On hearing it, many of His Disciples said, "This is a hard WORD, who can bear to listen to It?" 61 But *YESHUA*, aware that His Disciples were grumbling about this, said to them, "This is a trap for you? 62 Suppose you were to see the SON of Man going back up to where He was before? 63 It is Spirit who gives Life, the flesh is no help. The WORDS I have spoken to you are SPIRIT and Life, 64 yet some among you do not have faith." (For *YESHUA* knew from the outset which ones would not have faith in Him, also which one would betray Him.) 65 "This," He said, "Is why I told you that no one can come to Me unless the FATHER has made it possible for him."

6:66 From this time on, many of His Disciples turned back and no longer traveled around with Him. [Zechariah 13:8 "**...two portions will be cut off and perish, and the third will be left in it."** Isaiah 6:10 **"He has blinded their eyes and hardened their hearts, so that they do not see with their eyes, understand with their hearts, and repent, so that I could**

heal them."] 67 So *YESHUA* said to the Twelve, "Do you not want to leave too?" 68 Simon Peter answered Him, "LORD, to whom would we go? You have the WORD of Eternal Life. 69 We have faith, and we know that You are the Holy One of *ELOHIM*." 70 *YESHUA* answered them, "Did not I choose you, the Twelve? Yet one of you is an adversary." 71 (He was speaking of Judah, Son of Simon, from Iscariot; for this man; one of the Twelve! Was soon to betray Him.)

7:1 After this, *YESHUA* traveled around in the Galilee, intentionally avoiding Judea because the Jews were out to kill Him.

11:55 The *Appointed Time* of Passover was near, and many people went up from the country to *Yerushalayim* to perform the purification ceremony prior to Passover. 56 They were looking for *YESHUA*, and as they stood in the TEMPLE Courts they said to each other, "What do you think? That He simply would not come to the festival?" 57 Moreover, the head Priests and the Pharisees had given orders that anyone knowing *YESHUA'S* whereabouts should inform them, so that they could have Him arrested.

12:1 Six days before Passover, *YESHUA* came to Bethany, where Lazarus lived, the man *YESHUA* had raised from the dead; 2 so they gave a dinner there in His honor. Martha served the meal, and Lazarus was among those at the table with Him. 3 Mary took a whole pint of pure oil of spikenard, which is very expensive, poured it on *YESHUA'S* Feet and wiped His Feet with her hair, so that the house was filled with the fragrance of the perfume. 4 But one of the disciples, Judah from Iscariot, the one who was about to betray Him, said, 5 "This perfume is worth a year's wages! Why was not it sold and the money given to the poor?" 6 Now he said this not out of concern for the poor, but because he was a thief and he was in charge of the common purse and used to steal from it. 7 *YESHUA* said, "Leave her alone! She kept this for the day of My burial. 8 You always have the poor among you, but you will not always have Me."

9 A large crowd of Jews learned that He was there; and they came not only because of *YESHUA*, but also so that they could see Lazarus, whom He had raised from the dead. 10 The head Priests then decided to do away with Lazarus too, 11 since it was because of him that large numbers of the Jews were leaving their leaders and putting their faith in *YESHUA*.

2:13a It was almost time for the festival of Passover in Judea,

12:12 The next day, the large crowd that had come for the festival heard that *YESHUA* was on His way into *Yerushalayim*. 13 They took palm branches and went out to meet Him, shouting, Psalms 118:25 **"Deliver us!"** Psalms 118:26 **"Blessed is He who comes in the name of *ADONAI*, the KING of *Yisrael*!"** 14 After finding a donkey colt, *YESHUA* mounted it, just as the *Tanakh* says, 15 Zechariah 9:9 **"Daughter of Zion, do not be afraid! Look! Your KING is coming, sitting on a donkey's colt."**

[Witnesses: Matthew 21:4-11 "This happened in order to fulfill what had been spoken through the prophet, 5 '**Say to the Daughter of Zion,**' "**Look! Your KING is coming to you, riding humbly on a donkey, and on a colt, the offspring of a beast of burden!**" So the disciples went and did as *YESHUA* had directed them. 7 They brought the donkey and the colt and put their robes on them, and *YESHUA* sat on them. 8 Crowds of people carpeted the road with their clothing, while others cut branches from trees and spread them on the road. 9 The crowds ahead of him and behind shouted, '**Please! Deliver us!**' to the SON of David; '**Blessed is he who comes in the name of ADONAI!**' 'You in the highest heaven! **Please! Deliver us!**' When He entered *Yerushalayim*, the whole city was stirred. 'Who is this?' They asked. 11 And the crowds answered, 'This is *YESHUA*, the PROPHET from Nazareth in the Galilee." Mark 11:7-10 and Luke 19:32-38 repeat Matthew.]

12:16 His Disciples did not understand at first; but after *YESHUA* had been Glorified, then they remembered that the *Tanakh* said this about Him, and that they had done this for Him. 17 The group that had been with Him when He called Lazarus out of the tomb and raised him from the dead had been telling about it. 18 It was because of this too that the crowd came out to meet Him, they had heard that He had performed this miracle. 19 The Pharisees said to each other, "Look, you are getting nowhere! Why, the whole world has gone after Him!"

20 Among those who went up to worship at the festival were some Greek-speaking Jews. 21 They approached Philip, the

one from Bethsaida in the Galilee, with a request. "Sir," they said, "We would like to see *YESHUA*." 22 Philip came and told Andrew; then Andrew and Philip went and told *YESHUA*." 23 *YESHUA* gave them this answer: "The time has come for the SON of Man to be Glorified. 24 Yes, indeed! I tell you that unless a grain of wheat that falls to the ground dies, it stays just a grain; but it dies, it produces a big harvest. 25 He who loves his life loses it, but he who hates his life in this world will keep it safe right on into Eternal Life! 26 If someone is serving Me, let him follow Me; wherever I Am, My servant will be there too. My FATHER will honor anyone who serves Me.

27 "Now I Am in turmoil. What can I say, 'FATHER, save Me from this hour?' No, it was for this very reason that I have come to this hour. I will say this, 28 'FATHER, Glorify your NAME!'" At this a voice came out of Heaven, "I have Glorified it before, and I will Glorify it again!" 29 The crowd standing there and hearing it said that it had thundered; others said, "And angel spoke to Him." 30 *YESHUA* answered, "This voice did not come for My sake but for your. 31 Now is the time for this world to be judged, now the ruler of this world will be expelled. 32 As for Me, when I Am lifted up from the earth, I will draw everyone to Myself." 33 He said this to indicate what kind of death He would die.

34 The crowd answered, "We have learned from the *TORAH* that the MESSIAH remains forever. How is it that you say the SON of Man has to be 'Lifted up?' Who is this 'SON of Man?'" 35 *YESHUA* said to them, "The Light will be with you only a little while longer. Walk while you have the Light, or the dark will overtake you; he who walks in the dark does not know where he is going. 36 While you have the Light, put your faith in the Light, so that you may become People of the Light." *YESHUA* said these things, then went off and kept Himself hidden from them.

37 Even though He had performed so many miracles in their presence, they still did not put their faith in Him, 38 in order that what the prophet had said might be fulfilled, Isaiah 53:1 **"*ADONAI*, who has believed our report? To whom has the arm of *ADONAI* been revealed?"**

39 The reason they could not believe was as Isaiah 6:10 says, 40 **"He has blinded their eyes and hardened their hearts, so that they do not see with their eyes, understand with their hearts, and repent, so that I could heal them."**

41 (Isaiah said these things because he saw the DIVINE PRESENCE of *YESHUA* and spoke about Him.) 42 Nevertheless, many of the leaders did have faith in Him; but

because of the Pharisees they did not say so openly, out of fear of being banned from the Assembly 43 for they loved praise from other people more than praise from *ELOHIM.*

44 *YESHUA* declared publicly, "Those who put their faith in Me are trusting not merely in Me, but in the One who sent Me. 45 Also those who see Me see the One who sent Me. 46 I have come as a Light into the world, so that everyone who has faith in Me might not remain in the dark. 47 If anyone hears what I Am saying and does not observe it, I do not judge him; for I did not come to judge the world, but to save the world. 48 Those who reject Me and do not accept what I say have a judge; the WORD which I have spoken will judge them on the Last Day. 49. For I have not spoken on My Own initiative, but the FATHER who sent Me has given Me a Command namely, what to say and how to say it. 50 And I know that His Command is Eternal Life. So what I say is simply what the FATHER has told Me to say."

2:13b ...so *YESHUA* went up to *Yerushalayim.* 14 In the TEMPLE Grounds He found those who were selling cattle, sheep and pigeons, and others who were sitting at tables exchanging money. 15 He made a whip from cords and drove them all out of the TEMPLE Grounds, the sheep and cattle as well. He knocked over the money-changers' tables, scattering their coins; 16 and to the pigeon-sellers He said, "Get these things out of here! How dare you turn My FATHER'S House into a market?" 17 (His Disciples later recalled that the *Tanakh* says, Psalms 69:10(9) **"Zeal for your TEMPLE will devour Me."**)

[Witnesses: Matthew 21:12-13 *YESHUA* entered the TEMPLE Grounds and drove out those who were doing business there, both the merchants and their customers. He upset the desks of the money-changers and knocked over the benches of those who were selling pigeons. 13 He said to them, "It has been written, '**My TEMPLE will be called a *HOUSE* of prayer.**' But you are making it into a **den of robbers!**" Luke 19:45-46 repeats Matthew.] Showing that all three writings are about the same Passover event.

2:18 So the Jews confronted Him by asking Him, "What miraculous sign can You show us to prove You have the right to do all this?" 19 *YESHUA* answered them, "Destroy this

TEMPLE, and in three days I will raise it up again." 20 The Jews said, "It took 46 years to build this TEMPLE, and you are going to raise it in three days?" 21 But the "TEMPLE" He had spoken of was His Body. 22 Therefore, when He was raised from the dead, His Disciples remembered that He had said this, and they had faith in the *Tanakh* and in what *YESHUA* had said.

23 Now while *YESHUA* was in *Yerushalayim* at the Passover festival, there were many people who "Believed in His NAME" when they saw the miracles He performed. 24 But He did not commit Himself to them, for He knew what people are like; 25 that is, He did not need anyone to inform Him about a person, because He knew what was in the person's heart.

Passover *Seder*

13:1 It was just before the festival of Passover, and *YESHUA* knew that the time had come for Him to pass from this world to the FATHER. Having loved His Own people in the world, He loved them to the end. 2 They were at supper, and the Adversary had already put the desire to betray Him into the heart of Judah, Son of Simon from Iscariot. 3 *YESHUA* was aware that the FATHER had put everything in His Power, and that He had come from *ELOHIM* and was returning to *ELOHIM*. 4 So He rose from the table, removed His outer garments and wrapped a towel around His Waist. 5 Then He poured some water into a basin and began to wash the feet of the disciples and wipe them off with the towel wrapped around Him.

6 He came to Simon Peter, who said to Him, "LORD! You are washing my feet?" 7 *YESHUA* answered him, "You do not understand yet what I am doing, but in time you will understand." 8 "No!" said Peter, "You will never wash my feet!" *YESHUA* answered him, "If I do not wash you, you have

no share with Me." 9 "LORD," Simon Peter replied, "Not only my feet, but my hands and head too!" 10 *YESHUA* said to him, "A man who has had a bath does not need to wash, except his feet, his body is already clean. And you people are clean, but not all of you." 11 (He knew who was betraying Him; this is why He said, "Not all of you are clean.")

12 After He had washed their feet, taken back His clothes and returned to the table, He said to them, "Do you understand what I have done to you? 13 You call me *'RABBI'* and 'LORD,' and you are right, because I Am. 14 Now if I, the LORD and *RABBI*, have washed your feet, you also should wash each other's feet. 15 For I have set an example for you, so that you may do as I have done to you. 16 Yes, indeed! I tell you, a slave is not greater than his master, nor is an emissary greater than the one who sent him. 17 If you know these things, you will be blessed if you do them.

18 "I Am not talking to all of you, I know which ones I have chosen. But the Words of the *Tanakh* must be fulfilled that say, Psalms 41:10(9) **'The one eating My Bread has turned against Me.'** 19 I Am telling you now, before it happens; so that when it does happen, you may believe that I Am [who I say I Am]. 20 Yes, indeed! I tell you that a person who receives someone I send receives Me, and that anyone who

receives Me receives the One who sent Me."

21 After saying this, *YESHUA*, in deep anguish of Spirit, declared, "Yes, indeed! I tell you that one of you will betray Me." 22 The disciples stared at one another, totally mystified, whom could He mean? 23 One of His Disciples, the one *YESHUA* particularly loved, was reclining close beside Him. 24 So Simon Peter motioned to Him and said, "Ask which one He is talking about." 25 Leaning against *YESHUA'S* chest, He asked *YESHUA*, "LORD, who is it?" 26 *YESHUA* answered, "It is the one to whom I give this piece of unleavened bread after I dip it in the dish." So He dipped the piece of unleavened bread and gave it to Judah Son of Simon from Iscariot. 27 As soon as Judah took the piece of unleavened bread, the Adversary went into him. "What you are doing, do quickly!" *YESHUA* said to him. 28 But no one at the table understood why He had said this to him. 29 Some thought that since Judah was in charge of the common purse, *YESHUA* was telling him, "Buy what we need for the festival," or telling him to give something to the poor. 30 As soon as he had taken the piece of unleavened bread, Judah went out, and it was night.

31 After Judah had left, *YESHUA* said, "Now the SON of Man has been Glorified, and *ELOHIM* has been Glorified in Him. 32 If the SON has Glorified *ELOHIM*, *ELOHIM* will Himself

Glorify the SON, and will do so without delay. 33 Little children, I will be with you only a little longer. You will look for Me; and, as I said to the Jews, 'Where I Am going, you cannot come,' now I say it to you as well.

34 "I Am giving you a Command, that you keep on loving each other. In the same way that I have loved you, you are also to keep on loving each other. 35 Everyone will know that you are My Disciples by the fact that you have love for each other."

36 Simon Peter said to Him, "LORD, where are you going?" *YESHUA* answered, "Where I Am going, you cannot follow Me now; but you will follow later." 37 "LORD," Peter said to Him, "Why cannot I follow you now? I will lay down my life for You!" 38 *YESHUA* answered, "You will lay down your life for Me? Yes, indeed! I tell you, before the cock crows you will disown Me three times.

14:1 "Do not let yourselves be disturbed. Have faith in *ELOHIM* and faith in Me. 2 In My FATHER'S HOUSE are many places to live. If there were not, I would have told you; because I Am going there to prepare a place for you. 3 Since I Am going and preparing a place for you, I will return to take you with Me; so that where I Am, you may be also. 4

Furthermore, you know where I Am going; and you know the way there."

5 Thomas said to Him, "LORD, we do not know where you are going; so how can we know the way?" 6 *YESHUA* said, "I Am the Way and the Truth and the Life; no one comes to the FATHER except through Me. 7 Because you have known Me, you will also know My FATHER; from now on, you do know Him; in fact, you have seen Him."

8 Philip said to Him, "LORD, show us the FATHER, and it will be enough for us." 9 *YESHUA* replied to him, "Have I been with you so long without your knowing Me, Philip? Whoever has seen Me has seen the FATHER; so how can you say, 'show us the FATHER?' 10 Do you not believe that I Am united with the FATHER, and the FATHER united with Me? What I Am telling you, I Am not saying on My own initiative; the FATHER living in Me is doing His own works. 11 Have faith in Me, that I Am united with the FATHER, and the FATHER united with Me. But if you cannot, then have faith because of the works themselves. 12 Yes, indeed! I tell you that whoever has faith in Me will also do the works I do! Indeed, he will do greater ones, because I Am going to the FATHER. 13 In fact, whatever you ask for in My NAME, I will do; so that the FATHER may be Glorified in the SON. 14

If you ask Me for something in My NAME, I will do it.

15 "If you love Me, you will keep My Commands (*TORAH*); 16 and I will ask the FATHER, and He will give you another Comforting Counselor like Me, the SPIRIT of Truth, to be with you forever. 17 The world cannot receive Her, because it neither sees nor knows Her. You know Her, because She is staying with you and will be united with you. 18 I will not leave you orphans, I Am coming to you. 19 In just a little while, the world will no longer see Me; but you will see Me. Because I live, you too will live. 20 When that day comes, you will know that I Am united with My FATHER, and you with Me, and I with you. 21 Whoever has My Commands (*TORAH*) and keeps them is the one who loves Me, and the one who loves Me will be loved by My FATHER, and I will love him and reveal Myself to him."

22 Judah (not the one from Iscariot) said to Him, "What has happened, LORD, that You are about to reveal Yourself to us and not to the world?" 23 *YESHUA* answered him, "If someone loves Me, he will keep My WORD; and My FATHER will love him, and We will come to him and make Our Home with him. 24 Someone who does not love Me does not keep My WORDS, and the WORD you are hearing is not My Own but that of the FATHER who sent Me.

25 "I have told you these things while I Am still with you. 26 But the Counselor, the HOLY SPIRIT, whom the FATHER will send in My NAME, will teach you everything; that is, She will remind you of everything I have said to you.

27 "What I Am leaving with you is Peace and I Am giving you My Peace. I do not give the way the world gives. Do not let yourselves be upset or frightened. 28 You heard Me tell you, 'I Am leaving, and I will come back to you.' If you loved Me, you would have been glad that I Am going to the FATHER; because the FATHER is greater than I. 29 "Also, I have said it to you now, before it happens; so that when it does happen, you have faith.

30 "I will not be talking with you much longer, because the ruler of this world is coming. He has no claim on Me; 31 rather, this is happening so that the world may know that I love the FATHER, and that I do as the FATHER has commanded Me.

"Get up! Let's get going!"

15:1 "I Am the real Vine, and My FATHER is the Gardener. 2 Every branch which is part of Me but fails to bear fruit, He cuts off; and every branch that does bear fruit, He prunes, so that it may bear more fruit. 3 Right now, because of the WORD which I have spoken to you, you are pruned. 4 Stay united with Me, as I will with you; for just as the branch cannot put forth fruit by itself apart from the vine, so you cannot bear fruit apart from Me.

5 "I Am the Vine and you are the branches. Those who stay united with Me, and I with them, are the ones who bear much fruit; because apart from Me you cannot do a thing. 6 Unless a person remains united with Me, he is thrown away like a branch and dries up. Such branches are gathered and thrown into the fire, where they are burned up.

7 "If you remain united with me, and My WORDS with you, then ask whatever you want, and it will happen for you. 8 This is how My FATHER is glorified; in your bearing much fruit; this is how you prove to be My Disciples.

9 "Just as My FATHER has loved Me, I too have loved you; so stay in My Love. 10 If you keep My Commands, you will stay in My Love, just as I have kept My FATHER'S Commands and stay in His Love. 11 I have said this to you so that My Joy may be in you, and your joy be complete.

12 "This is My Command: that you keep on loving each other just as I have Loved you. 13 No one has greater love than a

person who lays down his life for his friends. 14 You are My Friends, if you do what I Command you. 15 I no longer call you slaves, because a slave does not know what his master is about; but I have called you Friends, because everything I have heard from My FATHER I have made known to you. 16 You did not choose Me, I chose you; and I have commissioned you to go and bear fruit, fruit that will last; so that whatever you ask from the FATHER in My NAME He may give you. 17 This is what I Command you, keep loving each other!

18 "If the world hates you, understand that it hated Me first. 19 If you belonged to the world, the world would have loved its own. But because you do not belong to the world and on the contrary, I have picked you out of the world and therefore the world hates you. 20 Remember what I told you, 'A slave is not greater than his master.' If they persecuted Me, they will persecute you too; if they kept My WORD, they will keep yours too. 21 But they will do all this to you on My account, because they do not know the One who sent Me.

22 "If I had not come and spoken to them, they would not be guilty of sin; but now, they have no excuse for their sin. 23 Whoever hates Me hates the FATHER also. 24 If I had not done in their presence works which no one else ever did, they would not be guilty of sin; but now, they have seen them and

have hated both Me and My FATHER. 25 But this has happened in order to fulfill the words in their *Torah* which read, Psalms 35:19, 69:5 **'They hated Me for no reason at all.'**

26 "When the Counselor comes, whom I will send you from the FATHER; the SPIRIT of Truth, who keeps going out from the FATHER; She will testify on My behalf. 27 And you willtestify too, because you have been with Me from the outset.

16:1 "I have told you these things so that you would not be caught by surprise. 2 They will ban you from the Assembly; in fact, the time will come when anyone who kills you will think he is serving *ELOHIM*! 3 They will do these things because they have understood neither the FATHER nor Me. 4 But I have told you this, so that when the time comes for it to happen, you will remember that I told you. I did not tell you this at first, because I was with you. 5 But now I Am going to the One who sent Me. "Not one of you is asking Me, 'Where are you going?' 6 Instead, because I have said these things to you, you are overcome with grief. 7 But I tell you the Truth, it is to your advantage that I go away; for if I do not go away, the Comforting Counselor will not come to you. However, if I do go, I will send Her to you.

8 "When She comes, She will show that the world is wrong about sin and about righteousness and about judgment; 9 about sin, in that people do not put their faith in Me; 10 about righteousness, in that I Am going to the FATHER and you will no longer see Me; 11 about judgment, in that the ruler of this world has been judged.

12 "I still have many things to tell you, but you cannot bear them now. 13 However, when the SPIRIT of Truth comes, She will guide you into all Truth; for She will not speak on Her Own initiative but will say only what She Hears. She will also announce to you the events of the future. 14 She will Glorify Me, because She will receive from what is Mine and announce it to you. 15 Everything the FATHER has is Mine; this is why I said that She receives from what is Mine and will announce it to you.

16 "In a little while, you will see Me no more; then, a little while later, you will see Me." 17 At this, some of the disciples said to one another, "What is this that He is telling us, 'In a little while, you would not see Me; then, a little while later, you will see Me'? And, 'I Am going to the FATHER'?" 18 They went on saying, "What is this 'Little while'? We do not

understand what He is talking about."

19 *YESHUA* knew that they wanted to ask Him, so He said to them, "Are you asking each other what I meant by saying, 'In a little while, you would not see Me; and then, a little while later, you will see Me?' 20 Yes, it is true. I tell you that you will sob and mourn, and the world will rejoice; you will grieve, but your grief will turn to joy. 21 When a woman is giving birth, she is in pain; because her time has come. But when the baby is born, she forgets her suffering out of joy that a child has come into the world. 22 So you do indeed feel grief now, but I Am going to see you again. Then your hearts will be full of joy, and no one will take your joy away from you.

23 "When that day comes, you would not ask anything of Me! Yes, indeed! I tell you that whatever you ask from the FATHER, He will give you in My NAME. 24 Till now you have not asked for anything in My NAME. Keep asking, and you will receive, so that your joy may be complete.

25 "I have said these things to you with the help of illustrations; however, a time is coming when I will no longer speak indirectly but will talk about the FATHER in plain language. 26 When that day comes, you will ask in My NAME. I Am not telling you that I will pray to the FATHER on your

behalf, 27 for the FATHER Himself loves you, because you have loved Me and have believed that I came from *ELOHIM*.

28 "I came from the FATHER and have come into the world; again, I Am leaving the world and returning to the FATHER."

29 The disciples said to him, "Look, You are talking plainly right now, You are not speaking indirectly at all. 30 Now we know that You know everything, and that You do not need to have people put their questions into words. This makes us believe that You came from *ELOHIM*."

31 *YESHUA* answered, "Now you do believe. 32 But a time is coming and indeed it has already come; when you will be scattered, each one looking out for himself; and you will leave Me all alone. Yet I Am not alone; because the FATHER is with Me.

33 "I have said these things to you so that, united with Me, you may have Peace. In the world, you have troubles. But be brave! I have conquered the world!"

17:1 After *YESHUA* had said these things, He looked up toward heaven and said, "FATHER, the time has come. Glorify Your SON, so that the SON may Glorify You; 2 just as You gave Him authority over all mankind, so that He might give Eternal Life to all those whom You have given Him. 3 And Eternal Life is this: to know You, the One True *ELOHIM*, and Him whom You sent, *YESHUA* the MESSIAH.

4 "I Glorified You on earth by finishing the work You gave Me to do. 5 Now, FATHER, Glorify Me alongside Yourself. Give Me the same Glory I had with You before the world existed.

6 "I made Your NAME known to the people You gave Me out of the world. They were Yours, You gave them to Me, and they have kept Your WORD. 7 Now they know that everything You have given Me is from You, 8 because the WORDS You gave Me I have given to them, and they have received them. They have really come to know that I came from You, and they have come to have faith that you sent Me.

9 "I Am praying for them. I Am not praying for the world, but for those you have given to Me, because they are Yours. 10 Indeed, all I have is Yours, and all You have is Mine, and in them I have been Glorified. 11 Now I Am no longer in the world. They are in the world, but I Am coming to You. HOLY FATHER, guard them by the power of Your NAME, which You have given to Me, so that they may be one, just as We are. 12 When I was with them, I guarded them by the power of

Your NAME, which You have given to Me; yes, I kept watch over them; and not one of them was destroyed (except the one meant for destruction, so that the *Tanakh* might be fulfilled). 13 But now, I Am coming to You; and I say these things while I Am still in the world so that they may have My Joy made complete in themselves.

14 "I have given them Your WORD, and the world hated them, because they do not belong to the world; just as I Myself do not belong to the world. 15 I do not ask You to take them out of the world, but to protect them from the Evil One. 16 They do not belong to the world, just as I do not belong to the world. 17 Set them apart for Holiness by means of the Truth for Your WORD is Truth. 18 Just as You sent Me into the world, I have sent them into the world. 19 On their behalf I Am setting Myself apart for Holiness, so that they too may be set apart for Holiness by means of the Truth.

20 "I pray not only for these, but also for those who will have faith in Me because of their word, 21 that they may all be one. Just as You, FATHER, are united with Me and I with You, I pray that they may be united with Us, so that the world may believe that You sent Me. 22 The Glory which You have given to Me, I have given to them; so that they may be one, just as We are One 23 and I Am united with them and You with Me,

so that they may be completely one, and the world thus realize that You sent Me, and that You have Loved them just as You have Loved Me.

24 "FATHER, I want those You have given Me to be with Me where I Am; so that they may see My GLORY, which You have given Me because You Loved Me before the creation of the world. 25 Righteous FATHER, the world has not known You, but I have known You, and these people have known that You sent Me. 26 I made Your NAME known to them, and I will continue to make it known; so that the Love with which You have Loved Me may be in them, and I Myself may be united with them."

18:1 After *YESHUA* had said all this, He went out with His Disciples across the stream that flows in winter through the Cedron Valley, to a spot where there was a grove of trees; and He and His Disciples went into it. 2 Now Judah, who was betraying Him, also knew the place; because *YESHUA* had often met there with His Disciples. 3 So Judah went there, taking with Him a detachment of Roman soldiers and some TEMPLE Guards provided by the head Priests and the Pharisees; they carried weapons, lanterns and torches. 4

YESHUA, who knew everything that was going to happen to Him, went out and asked them, "Whom do you want?" 5 "*YESHUA* from Nazareth," they answered. He said to them, "I Am." Also standing with them was Judah, the one who was betraying Him. 6 When He said, "I Am," they went backward from Him and fell to the ground. 7 So He inquired of them once more, "Whom do you want?" and they said, "*YESHUA* from Nazareth." 8 "I told you, 'I Am,'" answered *YESHUA*, "So if I Am the one you want, let these others go." 9 This happened so that what He had said might be fulfilled, "I have not lost one of those You gave Me."

10 Then Simon Peter, who had a sword, drew it and struck the slave of The High Priest, cutting off his right ear; the slave's name was Malchus. 11 *YESHUA* said to Peter, "Put your sword back in its scabbard! This is the cup the FATHER has given Me; am I not to drink it?"

12 So the detachment of Roman soldiers and their captain, together with the TEMPLE Guard of the Jews, arrested *YESHUA*, tied Him up, 13 and took Him first to 'Annas, the father-in-law of Caiaphas, who was The High Priest that fateful year. 14 (It was Caiaphas who had advised the Jews that it would be good for one man to die on behalf of the people.) 15 Simon Peter and another disciple followed *YESHUA*. The

second disciple was known to The High Priest, and he went with *YESHUA* into the courtyard of The High Priest; 16 but Peter stood outside by the gate. So the other disciple, the one known to The High Priest, went back out and spoke to the woman on duty at the gate, then brought Peter inside. 17 The woman at the gate said to Peter, "You are one of that Man's Disciples?" He said, "No, I am not." 18 Now the slaves and guards had lit a fire because it was cold, and they were standing around it warming themselves; Peter joined them and stood warming himself too.

19 The High Priest questioned *YESHUA* about His Disciples and about what He taught. 20 *YESHUA* answered, "I have spoken quite openly to everyone; I have always taught in an Assembly or in the TEMPLE where all Jews meet together, and I have said nothing in secret; 21 so why are you questioning Me? Question the ones who heard what I said to them; look, they know what I said." 22 At these words, one of the guards standing by slapped *YESHUA* in the face and said, "This is how You talk to the High Priest?" 23 *YESHUA* answered him, "If I said something wrong, state publicly what was wrong; but if I was right, why are you hitting Me?" 24 So 'Annas sent Him, still tied up, to Caiaphas The High Priest.

25 Meanwhile, Simon Peter was standing and warming

himself. They said to him, "Are not you also one of His Disciples?" He denied it, saying, "No, I am not." 26 One of the slaves of The High Priest, a relative of the man whose ear Peter had cut off, said, "Did not I see you with Him in the grove of trees?" 27 So again Peter denied it, and instantly a cock crowed. (Similar to a Town Crier)

28 They led YESHUA from Caiaphas to the governor's headquarters. By now it was early morning. They did not enter the headquarters building because they did not want to become ritually defiled and thus unable to eat the Passover meal. 29 So Pilate went outside to them and said, "What charge are you bringing against this Man?" 30 They answered, "If He had not done something wrong, we would not have brought Him to you." 31 Pilate said to them, "You take Him and judge Him according to your own law." The Jews replied, "We do not have the legal power to put anyone to death." 32 This was so that what YESHUA had said, about how He was going to die, might be fulfilled.

33 So Pilate went back into the headquarters, called YESHUA and said to Him, "Are you the KING of the Jews?" 34 YESHUA answered, "Are you asking this on your own, or have other people told you about Me?" 35 Pilate replied, "Am I a Jew? Your own nation and head Priests have handed You over

to me; what have You done?" 36 *YESHUA* answered, "My KINGDOM does not derive its authority from this world's order of things. If it did, My Men would have fought to keep Me from being arrested by the Jews. But My KINGDOM does not come from here." 37 "So then," Pilate said to Him, "You are a KING, after all." *YESHUA* answered, "You say I Am a KING. The reason I have been born, the reason I have come into the world, is to bear witness to the Truth. Every one who belongs to the Truth listens to Me." 38 Pilate asked him, "What is Truth?" Having said this, Pilate went outside again to the Jews and told them, "I do not find any case against Him. 39 However, you have a custom that at Passover I set one prisoner free. Do you want me to set free for you the 'KING of the Jews'?" 40 But they yelled back, "No, not this Man but *Bar-Abba*!" (*Yeshua Bar-Abba* was a revolutionary; verses *YESHUA BEN-ABBA*, SON of *ELOHIM*)

19:1 Pilate then took *YESHUA* and had Him flogged. 2 The soldiers twisted thorn-branches into a crown and placed it on

His Head, put a purple robe on Him, 3 and went up to Him, saying over and over, "Hail, 'KING of the Jews'!" and hitting Him in the face.

4 Pilate went outside once more and said to the crowd, "Look, I am bringing Him out to you to get you to understand that I find no case against Him." 5 So *YESHUA* came out, wearing the thorn-branch crown and the purple robe. Pilate said to them, "Look at the Man!" 6 When the head Priests and the TEMPLE Guards saw Him they shouted, "Put Him to death on the *stake*! Put Him to death on the *stake*!" Pilate said to them, "You take Him out yourselves and put Him to death on the *stake*, because I do not find any case against Him." 7 The Jews answered him, "We have a law; according to that law, He ought to be put to death, because He made Himself out to be the SON of *ELOHIM*." 8 On hearing this, Pilate became even more frightened.

9 He went back into the headquarters and asked *YESHUA*, "Where are You from?" But *YESHUA* did not answer. 10 So Pilate said to Him, "You refuse to speak to me? Do you not understand that it is in my power either to set You free or to have You executed on the *stake*?" 11 *YESHUA* answered, "You would have no power over Me if it had not been given to you from above; this is why the one who handed Me over to you is

guilty of a greater sin." 12 On hearing this, Pilate tried to find a way to set Him free; but the Jews shouted, "If you set this Man free, it means you are not a 'Friend of the Emperor'! Everyone who claims to be a King is opposing the Emperor!" 13 When Pilate heard what they were saying, he brought *YESHUA* outside and sat down on the judge's seat in the place called The Pavement, but in Hebrew *Gabbatha*; 14 it was about noon on *Preparation Day* for Passover (14th). He said to the Jews, "Here is your KING!" 15 They shouted, "Take Him away! Take Him away! Put Him to death on the *stake*!" Pilate said to them, "You want me to execute your KING on a *stake*?" The head Priests answered, "We have no king but the Emperor." 16 Then Pilate handed *YESHUA* over to them to have Him put to death on the *stake*. So they took charge of *YESHUA*. 17 Carrying the stake Himself He went out to the place called Skull (in Aramaic, *Gulgolta*). 18 There they nailed Him to the *stake* along with two others, one on either side, with *YESHUA* in the middle. 19 Pilate also had a notice written and posted on the stake; it read,

YESHUA FROM NATZERET ישוע מנצרת

THE KING OF THE JEWS המלך היהודם

20 Many of the Jews read this notice, because the place where

YESHUA was put on the *stake* was close to the city; and it had been written in Hebrew, in Latin and in Greek. 21 The Jews' head Priests therefore said to Pilate, "Do not write, 'The KING of the Jews,' but 'He said, "I Am KING of the Jews."'" 22 Pilate answered, "what I have written, I have written."

23 When the soldiers had nailed YESHUA to the *stake*, they took His clothes and divided them into four shares, a share for each soldier, with the under-robe left over. Now the under-robe was seamless, woven in one piece from top to bottom; 24 so they said to one another, "We should not tear it in pieces; let us cast lots for it." This happened in order to fulfill the Words from the *Tanakh*, "They divided My clothes among themselves Psalms 22:19 (18) **and gambled for My Robe.**" This is why the soldiers did these things.

25 Nearby YESHUA'S execution *stake* stood His Mother, His Mother's sister Mary the wife of Clopas, and Mary from Magdala. 26 When YESHUA saw His Mother and the disciple whom He loved standing there, He said to His Mother, "Mother, this is your son." 27 Then He said to the disciple, "This is your mother." And from that time on, the disciple took her into his own house.

28 After this, knowing that all things had accomplished their

purpose, *YESHUA*, in order to fulfill the Words of the *Tanakh*, said, "I Am thirsty." 29 A jar full of cheap sour wine was there; so they soaked a sponge in the wine, coated it with oregano leaves and held it up to His Mouth. 30 After *YESHUA* had taken the wine, He said, "It is accomplished!" And, letting His Head droop, He delivered up His Spirit.

31 It was *Preparation Day*, and the Jews did not want the bodies to remain on the *stake* on the Sabbath, since it was an especially important Sabbath, (First day of Unleavened Bread). So they asked Pilate to have the legs broken and the bodies removed. 32 The soldiers came and broke the legs of the first man who had been put on a *stake* beside *YESHUA*, then the legs of the other one; 33 but when they got to *YESHUA* and saw that He was already dead, they did not break His Legs. 34 However, one of the soldiers stabbed His Side with a spear, and at once Blood and Water flowed out. 35 The man who saw it has testified about it, and his testimony is true. And he knows that he tells the truth, so you too can have faith. 36 For these things happened in order to fulfill this passage of the *Tanakh*: Psalms 34:21 (20); Exodus 12:46; Numbers 9:12 **"Not one of His bones will be broken."** 37 And again, another passage says, Zechariah 12:10 **"They will look at Him whom they have pierced."**

38 After this, Joseph of Arimathea, who was a disciple of *YESHUA*, but a secret one out of fear of the Jews, asked Pilate if he could have *YESHUA'S* Body. Pilate gave his consent, so Joseph came and took the Body away. 39 Also Nicodemus, who at first had gone to see *YESHUA* by night, came with some seventy pounds of spices and a mixture of myrrh with aloes. 40 They took *YESHUA'S* Body and wrapped it up in linen sheets with the spices, in keeping with Jewish burial practice. 41 In the vicinity of where He had been executed was a garden, and in the garden was a new tomb in which no one had ever been buried. 42 So, because it was *Preparation Day* for the Jews, and because the tomb was close by, that is where they buried *YESHUA*.

20:1 Early on the '*first day of the week*' (going-out of the Sabbath), while it was still dark, Mary from Magdala went to the tomb and saw that the stone had been removed from the tomb. 2 So she came running to Simon Peter and the other disciple, the one *YESHUA* loved, and said to them, "They have taken the LORD out of the tomb, and we do not know where they have put Him!"

3 Then Peter and the other disciple started for the tomb. 4 They

both ran, but the other disciple out ran Peter and reached the tomb first. 5 Stooping down, he saw the linen burial-sheets lying there but did not go in. 6 Then, following him, Simon Peter arrived, entered the tomb and saw the burial-sheets lying there, 7 also the cloth that had been around His Head, lying not with the sheets but in a separate place and still folded up. 8 Then the other disciple, who had arrived at the tomb first, also went in; he saw, and he had faith. 9 (They had not yet come to understand that the *Tanakh* teaches that the MESSIAH has to rise from the dead.)

10 So the disciples returned home, 11 but Mary stood outside crying. As she cried, she bent down, peered into the tomb, 12 and saw two angels in white sitting where the body of YESHUA had been, one at the head and one at the feet. 13 "Why are you crying?" they asked her. "They took my LORD," she said to them, "And I do not know where they have put Him."

14 As she said this, she turned around and saw YESHUA standing there, but she did not know it was He. 15 YESHUA said to her, "Lady, why are you crying? Whom are you looking for?" Thinking He was the gardener, she said to Him, "Sir, if you are the one who carried Him away, just tell me where you put Him; and I will go and get Him myself." 16 YESHUA said

to her, "Mary!" Turning, she cried out to Him in Hebrew, "*Rabbani*!" (that is, "Teacher!") 17 "Stop holding onto Me," YESHUA said to her, "Because I have not yet gone back to the FATHER. But go to My Brothers, and tell them that I Am going back to My FATHER and your FATHER, to My *ELOHIM* and your *ELOHIM*." 18 Mary of Magdala went to the disciples with the news that she had seen the LORD and that He had told her this.

19 In the evening that same day, the first day of the week, when the disciples were gathered together behind locked doors out of fear of the Jews, YESHUA came, stood in the middle and said, "Peace be upon you!" 20 Having greeted them, He showed them His Hands and His Side. The disciples were overjoyed to see the LORD. 21 "Peace be upon you!" YESHUA repeated. "Just as the FATHER sent Me, I Myself am also sending you." 22 Having said this, He breathed on them and said to them, "Receive the HOLY SPIRIT! 23 If you forgive someone's sins, their sins are forgiven; if you hold them, they are held."

24 Now Thomas (the name means "twin"), one of the Twelve, was not with them when YESHUA came. 25 When the other disciples told him, "We have seen the LORD," he replied, "Unless I see the nail marks in His Hands, put my finger into

the place where the nails were and put my hand into His Side, I refuse to believe it."

26 A week later His Disciples were once more in the room, and this time Thomas was with them. Although the doors were locked, *YESHUA* came, stood among them and said, "Peace be upon you!" 27 Then He said to Thomas, "Put your finger here, look at My Hands, take your hand and put it into My Side. Do not be lacking in faith, but have faith!" 28 Thomas answered Him, "My LORD and My *ELOHIM*!" 29 *YESHUA* said to him, "Have you faith because you have seen Me? How blessed are those who do not see, but have faith anyway!"

30 In the presence of the disciples *YESHUA* performed many other miracles which have not been recorded in this book. 31 But these which have been recorded are here so that you may have faith that *YESHUA* is the MESSIAH, the SON of *ELOHIM*, and that by this faith you may have Life because of who He is.

21:1 After this, *YESHUA* appeared again to the disciples at Lake Kinneret. Here is how it happened: 2 Simon Peter and Thomas (his name means "twin") were together with Nathanael from Cana in the Galilee, the sons of Zebedee, and two other disciples. 3 Simon Peter said, "I am going fishing." They said to him, "We are coming with you." They went and got into the boat, but that night they did not catch anything. 4 However, just as day was breaking, *YESHUA* stood on shore, but the disciples did not know it was He. 5 He said to them, "You do not have any fish, do you?" "No," they answered Him. 6 He said to them, "Throw in your net to the right-side and you will catch some." So they threw in their net, and there were so many fish in it that they could not haul it aboard. 7 The disciple *YESHUA* loved said to Peter, "It is the LORD!" On hearing it was the LORD, Simon Peter threw on his coat, because he was stripped for work, and plunged into the lake; 8 but the other disciples followed in the boat, dragging the net full of fish; for they were not far from shore, only about a hundred yards. 9 When they stepped ashore, they saw a fire of burning coals with a fish on it, and some bread. 10 *YESHUA* said to them, "Bring some of the fish you have just caught." 11 Simon Peter went up and dragged the net ashore. It was full of fish, 153 of them; but even with so many, the net was not torn. 12 *YESHUA* said to them, "Come and have breakfast." None of the disciples dared to ask Him, "Who are You?" They knew it was the LORD. 13 *YESHUA* came, took the bread and gave it to them, and did the same with the fish. 14 This was now the third time

YESHUA had appeared to the disciples after being raised from the dead.

15 After breakfast, *YESHUA* said to Simon Peter, "Simon Son of John, do you love Me more than these?" He replied, "Yes, LORD, You know I am your friend." He said to him, "Feed My Lambs." 16 A second time He said to him, "Simon Son of John, do you love Me?" He replied, "Yes, LORD, You know I am Your friend." He said to him, "Shepherd My Sheep." 17 The third time He said to him, "Simon Son of John, are you My Friend?" Simon was hurt that He questioned him a third time: "Are you My Friend?" So he replied, "LORD, You know everything! You know I am Your Friend!" *YESHUA* said to him, "Feed My Sheep! 18 Yes, indeed! I tell you, when you were younger, you put on your clothes and went where you wanted. But when you grow old, you will stretch out your hands, and someone else will dress you and carry you where you do not want to go." 19 He said this to indicate the kind of death by which Peter would bring glory to *ELOHIM*. Then *YESHUA* said to him, "Follow Me!"

20 Peter turned and saw the disciple *YESHUA* especially loved following behind, the one who had leaned against Him at the supper and had asked, "Who is the one who is betraying You?" 21 On seeing him, Peter said to *YESHUA*, "LORD, what about

him?" 22 *YESHUA* said to him, "If I want him to stay on until I come, what is it to you? You, follow Me!" 23 Therefore the word spread among the brothers that this disciple would not die. However, *YESHUA* did not say he would not die, but simply, "If I want him to stay on until I come, what is it to you?"

24 This one is the disciple who is testifying about these things and who has recorded them. And we know that his testimony is true.

25 But there are also many other things *YESHUA* did; and if they were all to be recorded, I do not think the whole world could contain the books that would have to be written!

One Passover

	Matthew	Mark	Luke
John 2:13b-17	21:12-13	11:11a	19:45-46
John 6:1-13	14:13-21	6:34-44	9:11-17
John 6:16-21	14:22-34	6:45-53	
John 12:12-15	21:4-11	11:7-10	19:32-38
John 13:2	26:20-21A	14:17-18A	22:14-15
John 13:18, 21	26:21B	14:18B	
John 13:26-27	26:23		14:20

Leonard Rothenberger, Jr

THE GOSPEL OF JOHN

Three writings from the **B'rit HaChidaysh**

בְּרִית הָחֲדֵשׁ

"Covenant the Renewed"

Aka New Testament

This translations conforms as closely as possible to Biblical Hebrew

FIRST WRITING OF JOHN

1:1 In the beginning was the WORD/*TORAH*, and the WORD/*TORAH* was with *ELOHIM*, and the WORD/*TORAH* was *ELOHIM*. 2 He (*TORAH*/*YESHUA*/יהוה) was with *ELOHIM* in the beginning. 3 All things came to be through Him, and without Him nothing made had being. 4 In Him was Life, and the Life was the Light of mankind. 5 The Light shines in the darkness, and the darkness has not suppressed It.

6 There was a man sent from *ELOHIM* whose name was John. 7 He came to be a testimony, to bear witness concerning the Light; so that through Him, everyone might put his faith in *ELOHIM* and be faithful to Him. 8 He himself was not that Light; no, he came to bear witness concerning the Light.

9 This was the True Light, which gives Light to everyone entering the world. 10 He was in the world; the world came to be through Him; yet the world did not know Him. 11 He came to His Own Homeland, yet His Own People did not receive Him.

12 But to as many as did receive Him, to those who put their

faith in His Person and Power, He gave the right to become CHILDREN of *ELOHIM*, 13 not because of bloodline, physical impulse or human intention, but because of *ELOHIM*.

14 The WORD/*TORAH* became a human being and lived with us, and we saw His DIVINE PRESENCE, the DIVINE PRESENCE of the FATHER'S only SON, full of Grace and Truth.

15 John witnessed concerning Him when he cried out, "This is the Man I was talking about when I said, 'The One coming after me has come to rank ahead of me, because He existed before me.'"

16 We have all received from His Fullness, yes, Grace upon Grace. 17 For the (Written) *TORAH* was given through Moses; Grace and Truth came through *YESHUA* the MESSIAH the Living *TORAH*.

18 No one has ever seen *ELOHIM*; but the Only and Unique SON, who is identical with *ELOHIM* and is at the FATHER'S Side; He has made the FATHER known.

19 Here is John's testimony: when the Jews sent Priests and Levites from *Yerushalayim* to ask him, "Who are you?" 20 He was very straightforward and stated clearly, "I am not the MESSIAH." 21 "Then who are you?" They asked him. "Are

you Elijah?" "No, I am not," he said. "Are you 'the PROPHET,' the One we're expecting?" "No," he replied. 22 So they said to him, "Who are you? so that we can give an answer to the people who sent us. What do you have to say about yourself?" 23 He answered in the words of Isaiah 40:3 the prophet, "I am **The voice of someone crying out: 'In the wilderness make the way of *ADONAI* straight!'"**

24 Some of those who had been sent were Pharisees. 25 They asked him, "If you are neither the MESSIAH nor Elijah nor 'the PROPHET,' then why are you *immersing* people?" 26 To them John replied, "I am *immersing* people in Water, but among you is standing Someone whom you do not know. 27 He is the One coming after me; I am not good enough even to untie His Sandal!" 28 All this took place in Bethany east of the Jordan, where John was *immersing*.

29 The next day, John saw *YESHUA* coming toward him and said, "Look! *ELOHIM'S* LAMB! The One who is taking away the sin of the world! 30 This is the Man I was talking about when I said, 'After me is coming Someone who has to rank above me, because He existed before me.' 31 I myself did not know who He was, but the reason I came *immersing* with Water was so that He might be made known to *Yisrael*." 32 Then John gave this testimony: "I saw the SPIRIT coming

down from Heaven like a Dove, and remaining on Him. 33 I myself did not know who He was, but the One who sent me to *immerse* in Water said to me, 'The One on whom you see the SPIRIT descending and remaining, this is the One who *immerses* in the *HOLY SPIRIT.*' 34 And I have seen and borne witness that this is the SON of *ELOHIM.*" [*YESHUA* was "Born Again" at this time.]

35 The next day, John was again standing with two of his disciples. 36 On seeing *YESHUA* walking by, he said, "Look! *ELOHIM'S* LAMB!" 37 His two disciples heard him speaking, and they followed *YESHUA.* 38 *YESHUA* turned and saw them following Him, and He asked them, "What are you looking for?" They said to Him, "*RABBI!*" "Where are you staying?" 39 He said to them, "Come and see." So they went and saw where He was staying, and remained with Him the rest of the day; it was about four o'clock in the afternoon. 40 One of the two who had heard John and had followed *YESHUA* was Andrew the brother of Simon Peter.

41 The first thing he did was to find his brother Simon and tell him, "We have found the *MASHIACH!*" (The word means "One who has been Anointed.") 42 He took him to *YESHUA.* Looking at him, *YESHUA* said, "You are Simon Son of John; you will be known as Peter." (The name means "rock.")

43 The next day, having decided to leave for the Galilee, *YESHUA* found Philip and said, "Follow Me!" 44 Philip was from Bethsaida, the town where Andrew and Peter lived. 45 Philip found Nathanael and told him, "We have found the One that Moses wrote about in the *TORAH*, also the Prophets; it is *YESHUA*, SON of Joseph from Nazareth!" 46 Nathanael answered him, "Nazareth? Can anything good come from there?" "Come and see," Philip said to him. 47 *YESHUA* saw Nathanael coming toward Him and remarked about him, "Here is a true son of *Yisrael*; nothing false in him!" 48 Nathanael said to Him, "How do You know me?" *YESHUA* answered him, "Before Philip called you, when you were under the fig tree, I saw you." 49 Nathanael said, "*RABBI*, you are the SON of *ELOHIM*! You are the KING of *Yisrael*!" 50 *YESHUA* answered him, "You believe all this just because I told you I saw you under the fig tree? You will see greater things than that!" 51 Then He said to him, "Yes indeed! I tell you that you will see, Genesis 28:12 **Heaven** opened and **the Angels of *ELOHIM* going up and coming down** on the SON of Man!"

2:1 On the third day of the week, there was a wedding at Cana in the Galilee; and the mother of *YESHUA* was there. 2 *YESHUA* too was invited to the wedding, along with His

Disciples. 3 The wine ran out, and *YESHUA'S* Mother said to Him, "They have no more wine." 4 *YESHUA* replied, "Mother, why should that concern Me? Or you? My time has not come yet." 5 His Mother said to the servants, "Do whatever He tells you." 6 Now six stone water-jars were standing there for the Jewish ceremonial washings, each with a capacity of twenty or thirty gallons. 7 *YESHUA* told them, "Fill the jars with water," and they filled them to the brim. 8 He said, "Now draw some out, and take it to the man in charge of the banquet;" and they took it. 9 The man in charge tasted the water; it had now turned into wine! He did not know where it had come from, but the servants who had drawn the water knew. So he called the bridegroom 10 and said to him, "Everyone else serves the good wine first and the poorer wine after people have drunk freely. But you have kept the good wine until now!" 11 This, the first of *YESHUA'S* miraculous signs, He did at Cana in the Galilee; He manifested His Glory, and His Disciples came to have faith in Him. 12 Afterwards, He and His Mother and Brothers and His Disciples went down to Capernaum and stayed there a few days.

13 It was almost time for the festival of Passover in Judah, 13 so *YESHUA* went up to *Yerushalayim.* 14 In the TEMPLE Grounds He found those who were selling cattle, sheep and

pigeons, and others who were sitting at tables exchanging money. 15 He made a whip from cords and drove them all out of the TEMPLE Grounds, the sheep and cattle as well. He knocked over the money-changers' tables, scattering their coins; 16 and to the pigeon-sellers He said, "Get these things out of here! How dare you turn My FATHER'S HOUSE into a market?" 17 (His Disciples later recalled that the *Tanakh* says, Psalms 69:10(9) **"Zeal for your HOUSE will devour Me."**)

[Witnesses: Matthew 21:12-13 *YESHUA* entered the TEMPLE Grounds and drove out those who were doing business there, both the merchants and their customers. He upset the desks of the money-changers and knocked over the benches of those who were selling pigeons. 13 He said to them, "It has been written, '**My House will be called a House of prayer.**' But you are making it into a **den of robbers!**" Luke 19:45-46 repeats Matthew.] Showing that all three writings are about the same Passover event.

2:18 So the Jews confronted Him by asking Him, "What miraculous sign can You show us to prove You have the right to do all this?" 19 *YESHUA* answered them, "Destroy this TEMPLE, and in three days I will raise it up again." 20 The Jews said, "It took 46 years to build this TEMPLE, and you are going to raise it in three days?" 21 But the "TEMPLE" He had spoken of was His Body. 22 Therefore, when He was raised from the dead, His Disciples remembered that He had said this, and they had faith in the *Tanakh* and in what *YESHUA* had said.

23 Now while *YESHUA* was in *Yerushalayim* at the Passover festival, there were many people who "Believed in His NAME" when they saw the miracles He performed. 24 But He did not commit Himself to them, for He knew what people are like; 25 that is, He did not need anyone to inform Him about a person, because He knew what was in the person's heart.

This is the end of John's first writing and beginning of the second.

SECOND WRITING OF JOHN

3:1 There was a man among the Pharisees, named Nicodemus, who was a ruler of the Jews. 2 This man came to *YESHUA* by night and said to Him, "*RABBI*, we know it is from *ELOHIM* that You have come as a Teacher; for no one can do these miracles You perform unless *ELOHIM* is with Him." 3 "Yes, indeed," *YESHUA* answered him, "I tell you that unless a person is born again from above, he cannot see the KINGDOM of *ELOHIM*." 4 Nicodemus said to Him, "How can a grown man be 'born'? Can he go back into his mother's womb and be born a second time?" 5 *YESHUA* answered, "Yes, indeed, I tell you that unless a person is born from Living Waters and the SPIRIT, he cannot enter the KINGDOM of *ELOHIM*. 6 What is born from the flesh is flesh, and what is born from the SPIRIT is SPIRIT. 7 Stop being amazed at My telling you that you must be born again from above! 8 The wind blows where it wants to, and you hear its sound, but you don't know where it comes from or where it is going. That is how it is with everyone who has been born from the SPIRIT"

9 Nicodemus replied, "How can this happen?" 10 *YESHUA* answered him, "You hold the office of Teacher in *Yisrael*, and you do not know this? 11 Yes, indeed! I tell you that what we speak about, we know; and what we give evidence of, we have seen; but you people do not accept our evidence! 12 If you people do not believe Me when I tell you about the things of the world, how will you believe Me when I tell you about the things of Heaven? 13 No one has gone up into Heaven; there is only the One who has come down from Heaven, the SON of Man. 14 Just as Moses lifted up the serpent in the wilderness, so must the SON of Man be lifted up; 15 so that everyone who has faith in Him may have Eternal Life.

16 "For *ELOHIM* so loved the world that He gave His Only and Unique SON, so that everyone who has faith in Him may have Eternal Life, instead of being utterly destroyed. 17 For *ELOHIM* did not send the SON into the world to judge the world, but rather so that through Him, the world might be saved. 18 Those who have faith in Him are not judged; those who do not have faith have been judged already, in that they have not trusted in the One who is *ELOHIM'S* Only and Unique SON. 19 "Now this is the judgment: the Light has come into the world, but people loved the darkness rather than the Light. Why? Because their actions were wicked. 20 For

everyone who does evil things hates the Light and avoids it, so that his actions would not be exposed. 21 But everyone who does what is True comes to the Light, so that all may see that His actions are accomplished through *ELOHIM*."

22 After this, *YESHUA* and His Disciples went out into the countryside of Judea, where He stayed awhile with them witnessing people *immersing*. 23 John too was witnessing *immersions* at the spring of Aenon, near Salem, because there was plenty of water there; and people kept coming to *immerse*. 24 (This was before John's imprisonment.)

25 A discussion arose between some of John's disciples and a Jew about ceremonial washing; 26 and they came to John and said to him, "*Rabbi,* you know the Man who was with you on the other side of the Jordan, the One you spoke about? Well, here He is, witnessing *immersions* and everyone is going to Him!" 27 John answered, "No one can receive anything unless it has been given to him from Heaven. 28 You yourselves can confirm that I did not say I was the MESSIAH, but that I have been sent ahead of Him. 29 The Bridegroom is the One who has the Bride; but the Bridegroom's Friend, who stands and listens to Him, is overjoyed at the sound of the Bridegroom's Voice. So this joy of mine is now complete. 30 He must become more important, while I become less important.

31 "He who comes from above is above all. He who is from the earth is from the earth and talks from an earthly point of view; He who comes from Heaven is above all. 32 He testifies about what He has actually seen and heard, yet no one accepts what He says! 33 Whoever does accept what He says puts his seal on the fact that *ELOHIM* is True, 34 because the One whom *ELOHIM* sent speaks *ELOHIM'S* WORDS. For *ELOHIM* does not give Him the Spirit in limited degree; 35 the FATHER loves the SON and has put everything in His Hands. 36 Whoever has faith in the SON has Eternal Life. But whoever disobeys the SON will not see that Life but remains subject to *ELOHIM'S* Wrath."

4:1 When *YESHUA* learned that the Pharisees had heard He was making more Disciples and witnessing more *immersions* than John 2 (although it was not *YESHUA* Himself who witnessing *immersions* but His Disciples), 3 *YESHUA* left Judea and set out again for the Galilee. 4 This meant that He had to pass through Samaria.

5 He came to a town in Samaria called Shechem, near the field Jacob had given to his son Joseph. 6 Jacob's well was there; so *YESHUA*, exhausted from His travel, sat down by the well; it was about noon. 7 A woman from Samaria came to draw some water; and *YESHUA* said to her, "Give Me a drink of water." 8

(His Disciples had gone into town to buy food.) 9 The woman from Samaria said to Him, "How is it that You, a Jew, ask for water from me, a woman of Samaria?" (For Jews do not associate with people from Samaria.) 10 *YESHUA* answered her, "If you knew *ELOHIM'S* Gift, that is, who it is saying to you, 'Give Me a drink of water,' then you would have asked Him; and He would have given you Living Water."

11 She said to Him, "Sir, you do not have a bucket, and the well is deep; so where do you get this 'Living Water'? 12 You are not greater than our father Jacob, are You? He gave us this well and drank from it, and so did his sons and his cattle." 13 *YESHUA* answered, "Everyone who drinks this water will get thirsty again, 14 but whoever drinks the Water I will give him will never be thirsty again! On the contrary, the Water I give him will become a Spring of Water inside him, welling up into Eternal Life!"

15 "Sir, give me this Water," the woman said to Him, "So that I would not have to be thirsty and keep coming here to draw water." 16 He said to her, "Go, call your husband, and come back." 17 She answered, "I do not have a husband." *YESHUA* said to her, "You are right, you do not have a husband! 18 You have had five husbands in the past, and you are not married to the man you are living with now! You have spoken the truth!"

19 "Sir, I can see that You are a Prophet," the woman replied. 20 "Our fathers worshipped on this mountain, but you people say that the place where one has to worship is in *Yerushalayim*." 21 *YESHUA* said, "Lady, believe me, the time is coming when you will worship the FATHER neither on this mountain nor in *Yerushalayim*. 22 You people do not know what you are worshipping; we worship what we do know, because salvation comes from the Jews. 23 But the time is coming; indeed, it is here now; when the true worshippers will worship the FATHER spiritually and truly, for these are the kind of people the FATHER wants worshipping Him. 24 *ELOHIM* is SPIRIT; and worshippers must worship Him spiritually and truly."

25 The woman replied, "I know that *MASHIACH* is coming" (that is, "The one who has been anointed"). "When He comes, He will tell us everything." 26 *YESHUA* said to her, "I, the person speaking to you, Am He."

27 Just then, His Disciples arrived. They were amazed that He was talking with a woman; but none of them said, "What do you want?" or, "Why are You talking with her?" 28 So the woman left her water-jar, went back to the town and said to the people there, 29 "Come, see a Man who told me everything I have ever done. Could it be that this is the MESSIAH?" 30

They left the town and began coming toward Him.

31 Meanwhile, the disciples were urging YESHUA, "RABBI, eat something." 32 But He answered, "I have food to eat that you do not know about." 33 At this, the disciples asked one another, "Could someone have brought Him food?" 34 YESHUA said to them, "My food is to do what the One who sent Me wants and to bring His Work to completion. 35 Do you not have a saying, 'Four more months and then the harvest?' Well, what I say to you is: open your eyes and look at the fields! They are already ripe for harvest! 36 The one who reaps receives his wages and gathers fruit for Eternal Life, so that the reaper and the sower may be glad together; 37 for in this matter, the proverb, 'One sows and another reaps,' holds true. 38 I sent you to reap what you have not worked for. Others have done the hard labor, and you have benefited from their work."

39 Many people from that town in Samaria put their faith in Him because of the woman's testimony, "He told me all the things I did." 40 So when these people from Samaria came to Him, they asked Him to stay with them. He stayed two days, 41 and many more came to faith because of what He said. 42 They said to the woman, "We no longer have faith because of what you said, because we have heard for ourselves. We know

indeed that this Man really is the Savior of the World."

43 After the two days, He went on from there toward the Galilee. 44 Now *YESHUA* Himself said, "A Prophet is not respected in His Own country." 45 But when He arrived in the Galilee, the people there welcomed Him, because they had seen all He had done at the festival in *Yerushalayim*; since they had been there too.

46 He went again to Cana in the Galilee, where He had turned the water into wine. An officer in the Royal Service was there; his son was ill in Capernaum. 47 This man, on hearing that *YESHUA* had come from Judea to the Galilee, went and asked Him to come down and heal his son, for he was at the point of death. 48 *YESHUA* answered, "Unless you people see signs and miracles, you simply will not have faith!" 49 The officer said to Him, "Sir, come down before my child dies." 50 *YESHUA* replied, "You may go, your son is alive." The man believed what *YESHUA* said and left. 51 As he was going down, his servants met him with the news that his son was alive 52 So he asked them at what time he had gotten better; and they said, "The fever left him yesterday at one o'clock in the afternoon." 53 The father knew that it was the very hour when *YESHUA* had told him, "Your son is alive;" and he and all his household had faith. 54 This was a second sign that

YESHUA did; He did it after He had come from Judea into the Galilee.

5:1 After this, was one of *YAHVEH'S Appointed Times* and *YESHUA* went up to *Yerushalayim*. 2 In *Yerushalayim*, by the Sheep Gate, is a pool called in Aramaic, Bethzatha, 3 in which lay a crowd of invalids: blind and lame and crippled. 4* 5 One man was there who had been ill for thirty-eight years. 6 *YESHUA*, seeing this man and knowing that he had been there a long time, said to him, "Do you want to be healed?" 7 The sick man answered, "I have no one to put me in the pool when the water is disturbed; and while I am trying to get there, someone goes ahead of me." 8 *YESHUA* said to him, "Get up, pick up your mat and walk!" 9 Immediately the man was healed, and he picked up his mat and walked. Now that day was Sabbath, 10 so the Jews said to the man who had been healed, "it is Sabbath! It's against the *TORAH* for you to carry your mat!" 11 But he answered them, "The Man who healed me, He is the One who told me, 'Pick up your mat and walk.'" 12 They asked him, "Who is the Man who told you to pick it up and walk?" 13 But the man who had been healed did not know who It was, because *YESHUA* had slipped away into the crowd.

4* Some manuscripts have verses 3b-4…waiting for the water to move; 4 for at certain times an angel of *ADONAI* went down into the pool and disturbed the water, and whoever stepped into the water first after it was disturbed was healed of whatever disease he had.

14 Afterwards *YESHUA* found him in the TEMPLE Court and said to him, "See, you are well! Now stop sinning, or something worse may happen to you!" 15 The man went off and told the Jews it was *YESHUA* who had healed him; 16 and on account of this, the Jews began harassing *YESHUA* because He did these things on the Sabbath.

17 But He answered them, "My FATHER has been working until now, and I, too, am working." 18 This answer made the Jews all the more intent on killing Him; not only was He breaking the Sabbath; but also, by saying that *ELOHIM* was His Own FATHER, He was claiming equality with *ELOHIM*. 19 Therefore, *YESHUA* said to them: "Yes, indeed! I tell you that the SON cannot do anything on His own, but only what He sees the FATHER doing; whatever the FATHER does, the SON does, too.

20 For the FATHER loves the SON and shows Him everything He does; and will show Him even greater things than these, so

that you will be amazed. 21. Just as the FATHER raises the dead and makes them alive, so too the SON makes alive anyone He wants. 22 The FATHER does not Judge anyone but has entrusted all Judgment to the SON, 23 so that all may honor the SON as they honor the FATHER. Whoever fails to honor the SON is not honoring the FATHER who sent Him. 24 Yes, indeed! I tell you that whoever hears what I Am saying and has faith in the One who sent Me has Eternal Life; that is, he will not come up for Judgment but has already crossed over from death to Life! 25 Yes, indeed I tell you that there is coming a time; in fact, it is already here; when the dead will hear the Voice of the SON of *ELOHIM*, and those who listen will come to Life. 26 For just as the FATHER has Life in Himself, so He has given the SON Life to have Himself. 27 Also He has given Him Authority to execute Judgment, because He is the SON of Man. 28 Do not be surprised at this; because the time is coming when all who are in the grave will hear His Voice 29 and come out; those who have done good to a Resurrection of Life, and those who have done evil to a Resurrection of Judgment. 30 I cannot do a thing on My Own. As I hear, I Judge; and My Judgment is right; because I do not seek My Own desire, but the desire of the One who sent Me.

31 "If I testify on My Own behalf, My Testimony is not valid.

32 But there is someone else testifying on My behalf, and I know that the Testimony He is making is valid; 33 you have sent to John, and he has testified to the Truth. 34 Not that I collect human testimony; rather, I say these things so that you might be saved. 35 He was a lamp burning and shining, and for a little while you were willing to bask in his light.

36 "But I have a Testimony that is greater than John's. For the things the FATHER has given Me to do, the very things I Am doing now, testify on My behalf that the FATHER has sent Me.

37 "In addition, the FATHER who sent Me has Himself Testified on My behalf. But you have never heard His Voice or seen His Shape; 38 moreover, His WORD does not stay in you, because you do not have faith in the One He sent. 39 You keep examining the *Tanakh* because you think that in it you have Eternal Life. Those very Scriptures bear witness to Me, 40 but you would not come to Me in order to have Life!

41 "I do not collect praise from men, 42 but I do know you people; I know that you have no love for *ELOHIM* in you! 43 I have come in My FATHER'S NAME, and you do not accept Me; if someone else comes in his own name, him you will accept. 44 How can you have faith? You are busy collecting

praise from each other, instead of seeking praise from *ELOHIM* only.

45 "But do not think that it is I who will be your accuser before the FATHER. Do you know who will accuse you? Moses, the very one you have counted on! 46 For if you really believed Moses, you would believe Me; because it was about Me that he wrote. 47 But if you do not believe what he wrote, how are you going to believe what I say?"

6:1 Sometime later, *YESHUA* went over to the far side of Lake Kinneret, 2 and a large crowd followed Him, because they had seen the miracles He had performed on the sick. 3 *YESHUA* went up into the hills and sat down there with His Disciples. 4 Now *YAHVEH'S Appointed Time* of Passover was coming up; 5 so when *YESHUA* looked up and saw that a large crowd was approaching, He said to Philip, "Where will we be able to buy bread, so that these people can eat?" 6 (Now *YESHUA* said this to test Philip, for *YESHUA* Himself knew what He was about to do.) 7 Philip answered, "Half a year's wages would not buy enough bread for them, each one would get only a bite!" 8 One of the disciples, Andrew the brother of Simon Peter, said to Him, 9 "There is a young fellow here who has five loaves of barley bread and two fish. But how far will they go among so many?"

10 *YESHUA* said, "Have the people sit down." There was a lot of grass there, so they sat down. The number of men was about five thousand. 11 Then *YESHUA* took the loaves of bread, and, after saying a Blessing, *(Baruch atah Adonai Elo-hai-nu Melek ha'olam ha-motzi lechem min ha-arets.* AH-MAYN. Blessed are You, *ADONAI*, our *ELOHIM*, Ruler of the universe, who brings bread from out of the earth.) gave to all who were sitting there, and likewise with the fish, as much as they wanted. 12 After they had eaten their fill, He told His Disciples, "Gather the leftover pieces, so that nothing gets wasted." 13 They gathered them and filled twelve baskets with the pieces from the five barley loaves left by those who had eaten.

[Witnesses: Matthew 14:13-21 "On hearing about this, *YESHUA* left in a boat to be by Himself in the wilderness. But the people learned of it and followed Him from the towns by land. 14 So when He came ashore, He saw a huge crowd; and, filled with compassion for them, He healed those of them who were sick. 15 As evening approached, the disciples came to Him and said, 'This is a remote place and it is getting late.

Send the crowds away, so that they can go and buy food for themselves in the villages.' 16 But *YESHUA* replied, 'They do not need to go away. Give them something to eat, yourselves!' 17 'All we have with us,' they said 'Is five loaves of bread and two fish.' 18 He said, 'Bring them here to Me.' 19 After instructing the crowds to sit down on the grass, He took the five loaves and the two fish and, looking up to Heaven, said a Blessing. Then He broke the loaves and gave them to the disciples, who gave them to the crowds. 20 They all ate as much as they wanted, and they took up twelve baskets full of pieces left over. 21 Those eating numbered about five thousand men, plus women and children. Mark 6:34-44 and Luke 9:11-17 repeat Matthew.]

6:14 When the people saw the miracle He had performed, they said, "This has to be 'The PROPHET' who is supposed to come into the world." 15 *YESHUA* knew that they were on the point of coming and seizing Him, in order to make Him King so He went back to the hills again. This time He went by Himself.

16 When evening came, His Disciples went down to the lake, 17 got into a boat and set out across the lake toward

Capernaum. By now it was dark, *YESHUA* had not yet joined them, 18 and the sea was getting rough, because a strong wind was blowing. 19 They had rowed three or four miles when they saw *YESHUA* approaching the boat, walking on the lake! They were terrified; 20 but He said to them, "Stop being afraid, it is I." 21 Then they were willing to take Him into the boat, and instantly the boat reached the land they were heading for.

[Witnesses: Matthew 14:22-34 "Immediately He had the disciples get in the boat and go on ahead of Him to the other side, while He sent the crowds away. 23 After He had sent the crowds away, He went up into the hills by Himself to pray. Night came on, and He was there alone. 24 But by this time, the boat was several miles from shore, battling a rough sea and a headwind. 25 Around four o'clock in the morning, He came toward them, walking on the lake! 26 When the disciples saw Him walking on the lake, they were terrified. 'It is a ghost!' They said and screamed with fear. 27 But at once *YESHUA* spoke to them. 'Courage,' He said, 'it is I. Stop being afraid.' 28 Then Peter called to Him, 'LORD, if it is really You, tell me to come to You on the water.' 29 'Come!' He said. So Peter got out of the boat and walked on the water toward *YESHUA*.

30 But when he saw the wind, he became afraid; and as he began to sink, he yelled, 'LORD! Save me!' 31 *YESHUA* immediately stretched out His hand, took hold of him, and said to him, 'Such little faith! Why did you doubt?' 32 As they went up into the boat, the wind ceased. 33 The men in the boat fell down before Him and exclaimed, 'You really are *ELOHIM'S SON!*' Having made the crossing, they landed at Gennesaret." Mark 6:45-53 repeats Matthew.]

6:22 The next day, the crowd which had stayed on the other side of the lake noticed that there had been only one boat there, and that *YESHUA* had not entered the boat with His Disciples, but that the disciples had been alone when they sailed off. 23 Then other boats, from Tiberias, came ashore near the place where they had eaten the bread after the LORD had said a Blessing. 24 Accordingly, when the crowd saw that neither *YESHUA* nor His Disciples were there, they themselves boarded the boats and made for Capernaum in search of *YESHUA*.

25 When they found Him on the other side of the lake, they asked Him, "*RABBI*, when did you get here?" 26 *YESHUA* answered, "Yes, indeed! I tell you, you are not looking for Me

because you saw miraculous signs, but because you ate the bread and had all you wanted! 27 Do not work for the food which passes away but for the food that stays on into Eternal Life, which the SON of Man will give you. For this is the One on whom *ELOHIM* the FATHER has put His Seal."

28 So they said to Him, "what should we do in order to perform the Works of *ELOHIM*?" 29 *YESHUA* answered, "Here is what the Work of *ELOHIM* is: to have faith in the One He sent!"

30 They said to Him, well, what miracle will You do for us, so that we may see it and have faith in You? What work can You perform? 31 Our fathers ate manna in the wilderness, as it says in the *Tanakh*, Psalms 78:24 and Nehemiah 9:15, '**He gave them Bread from Heaven** to eat.' 32 *YESHUA* said to them, "Yes, indeed! I tell you it was not Moses who gave the Bread from Heaven; 33 for *ELOHIM'S* Bread is the One who comes down out of Heaven and gives Life to the world."

34 They said to Him, "Sir, give us this Bread from now on." 35 *YESHUA* answered, "I Am the Bread which is Life! Whoever comes to Me will never go hungry, and whoever has faith in Me will never be thirsty. 36 I told you that you have seen but still do not have faith. 37 Everyone the FATHER gives Me will

come to Me, and whoever comes to Me I will certainly not turn away. 38 For I have come down from Heaven not to do My Own Will but the Will of the One who sent Me. 39 And this is the will of the One who sent Me: that I should not lose any of all those He has given Me, but, should raise them up in the Last Days. 40 Yes, this is the Will of My FATHER: that all who see the SON and have faith in Him should have Eternal Life, and that I should raise him up in the Last Days."

41 At this the Jews began grumbling about Him because He said, "I Am the Bread which has come down from Heaven." 42 They said, "Is not this *YESHUA* SON of Joseph? We know His Father and Mother! How can He now say, I have come down from Heaven?'" 43 *YESHUA* answered them, "Stop grumbling to each other! 44 No one can come to Me unless the FATHER; the One who sent Me; draws him. And I will raise him up in the Last Days. 45 It is written in the Prophets, Isaiah 54:13 **'They will all be taught by *ADONAI*.'** Everyone who listens to the FATHER and learns from Him comes to Me. 46 Not that anyone has seen the FATHER except the One who is from *ELOHIM*, He has seen the FATHER. 47 Yes, indeed! I tell you, whoever has faith has Eternal Life: 48 I Am the Bread which is Life. 49 Your fathers ate manna in the wilderness; they died. 50 But the Bread that has come down from Heaven

is such that a person may eat It and not die. 51 I Am the Living Bread that has come down from Heaven; if anyone eats this Bread, he will live forever. Furthermore, the Bread that I will give is My Own Flesh; and I will give it for the Life of the world."

52 At this, the Jews disputed with one another, saying, "How can this Man give us His Flesh to eat?" 53 Then *YESHUA* said to them, "Yes, indeed! I tell you that unless you eat the Flesh of the SON of Man and drink His Blood, you do not have life in yourselves. 54 Whoever eats My Flesh and drinks My Blood has Eternal Life; that is, I will raise him up in the Last Days. 55 For My Flesh is True Food, and My Blood is True Drink. 56 Whoever eats My Flesh and drinks My Blood lives in Me, and I live in him. 57 Just as the living FATHER sent Me, and I live through the FATHER, so also whoever eats Me will live through Me. 58 So this is the Bread that has come down from Heaven; it is not like the bread the fathers ate; they are dead, but whoever eats this Bread will Live Forever!" 59 He said these things as He was teaching in an Assembly in Capernaum.

60 On hearing it, many of His Disciples said, "This is a hard Word, who can bear to listen to It?" 61 But *YESHUA*, aware that His Disciples were grumbling about this, said to them, "This is a trap for you? 62 Suppose you were to see the SON of

Man going back up to where He was before? 63 It is Spirit who gives Life, the flesh is no help. The WORDS I have spoken to you are SPIRIT and Life, 64 yet some among you do not have faith." (For *YESHUA* knew from the outset which ones would not have faith in Him, also which one would betray Him.) 65 "This," He said, "Is why I told you that no one can come to Me unless the FATHER has made it possible for him."

6:66 From this time on, many of His Disciples turned back and no longer traveled around with Him. [Zechariah 13:8 **"...two portions will be cut off and perish, and the third will be left in it."** Isaiah 6:10 **"He has blinded their eyes and hardened their hearts, so that they do not see with their eyes, understand with their hearts, and repent, so that I could heal them."**] 67 So *YESHUA* said to the Twelve, "Do you not want to leave too?" 68 Simon Peter answered Him, "LORD, to whom would we go? You have the WORD of Eternal Life. 69 We have faith, and we know that You are the HOLY One of *ELOHIM*." 70 *YESHUA* answered them, "Did not I choose you, the Twelve? Yet one of you is an adversary." 71 (He was speaking of Judah Son of Simon, from Iscariot; for this man; one of the Twelve! Was soon to betray Him.)

7:1 After this, *YESHUA* traveled around in the Galilee, intentionally avoiding Judea because the Jews were out to kill Him.

This is the end of the second writing of John and the beginning of the third and his final writing in the Gospels.

Between verse 6:71 and verse 7:2 there is a time span of six months here if John's writings are in order.

Third Writing of John

7:2 But the festival of Tabernacle in Judea was near; 3 so His Brothers said to Him, "Leave here and go into Judea, so that Your Disciples can see the miracles You do; 4 for no one who wants to become known acts in secret. If You are doing these things, show Yourself to the world!" 5 (His Brothers spoke this way because they had not put their faith in Him.) 6 *YESHUA* said to them, "My time has not yet come; but for you, any time is right. 7 The world cannot hate you, but it does hate Me, because I keep telling it how wicked its ways are. 8 You, go on up to the festival; as for Me, I Am not going up to this festival now, because the right time for Me has not yet come." 9 Having said this, He stayed on in the Galilee.

10 But after His Brothers had gone up to the festival, He too went up, not publicly but in secret. 11 At the festival, the Jews were looking for Him. "Where is He?" They asked. 12 And among the crowds there was much whispering about Him. Some said, "He is a good Man;" but others said, "No, He is deceiving the masses." 13 However, no one spoke about Him

openly, for fear of the Jews.

14 Not until the festival was half over did *YESHUA* go up to the TEMPLE Courts and begin to teach. 15 The Jews were surprised: "How does this man know so much without having studied?" they asked. 16 So *YESHUA* gave them an answer: "My Teaching is not My Own, it comes from the One who sent Me. 17 If anyone wants to do His Will, he will know whether My Teaching is from *ELOHIM* or I speak on My Own. 18 A person who speaks on his own is trying to win praise for himself; but a person who tries to win praise for the One who sent Him is Honest, there is nothing false about Him. 19 Did not Moses give you the *TORAH*? Yet not one of you obeys the *TORAH*! Why are you out to kill Me?" 20 "You have a *demon!*" the crowd answered. "Who is out to kill You?" 21 *YESHUA* answered them, "I did one thing; and because of this, all of you are amazed. 22 Moses gave you circumcision and not that it came from Moses but from the Patriarchs, and you do a boy's circumcision on the Sabbath. 23 If a boy is circumcised on the Sabbath so that the *TORAH* of Moses will not be broken, why are you angry with Me because I made a man's whole body well on the Sabbath? 24 Stop judging by surface appearances, and judge the right way!"

25 Some of the *Yerushalayim* people said, "Is not this the Man

they are out to kill? 26 Yet here He is, speaking openly; and they do not say anything to Him. Could it be, that the authorities have actually concluded He is the MESSIAH? 27 But, we know where this Man comes from; but when the MESSIAH comes, no one will know where He comes from." 28 Whereupon *YESHUA*, continuing to teach in the TEMPLE Courts, cried out, "Indeed you do know Me! And you know where I Am from! And I have not come on My Own! The One who sent Me is real. But Him you do not know! 29 I do know Him, because I Am with Him, and He sent Me!"

30 At this, they tried to arrest Him; but no one laid a hand on Him; because His time had not yet come. 31 However, many in the crowd put their faith in Him and said, "When the MESSIAH comes, will He do more miracles than this Man has done?"

32 The Pharisees heard the crowd whispering these things about *YESHUA*; so the head Priests and the Pharisees sent some of the TEMPLE Guards to arrest Him. 33 *YESHUA* said, "I will be with you only a little while longer; then I will go away to the One who sent Me. 34 You will look for Me and not find Me; indeed, where I Am, you cannot come." 35 The Jews said to themselves, "Where is this Man about to go, that we would not find Him? Does He intend to go to the Greek

Diaspora and teach the Greek-speaking Jews? 36 And when He says, 'You will look for Me and not find Me; indeed, where I Am, you cannot come.

37 Now on the last day of the festival of Tabernacle, the greatest day, *YESHUA* stood and cried out, "If anyone is thirsty, let him keep coming to Me and drinking! 38 Whoever puts his faith in Me, as the Scripture says, rivers of Living Waters will flow from his inmost being!" 39 (Now He said this about the SPIRIT, whom put their faith in Him were to receive later; the SPIRIT had not yet been given, because *YESHUA* had not yet been Glorified.)

40 On hearing His WORDS, some people in the crowd said, "Surely this Man is 'the PROPHET;'" 41 others said, "This is the MESSIAH." But others said, "How can the MESSIAH come from the Galilee? 42 Does not the *Tanakh* say that the MESSIAH is from **the seed of David** II Samuel 7:12, and comes **from Bethlehem,** Micah 5:1 (2), the village where David lived?" 43 So the people were divided because of Him. 44 Some wanted to arrest Him, but no one laid a hand on Him.

45 The guards came back to the head Priests and the Pharisees, who asked them, "Why did not you bring Him in?" 46 The guards replied, "No one ever spoke the way this Man speaks!"

47 "You mean you have been taken in as well?" the Pharisees retorted. 48 "Has any of the authorities trusted Him? Or any of the Pharisees? No! 49 True, these people of the land do, but they know nothing about the *TORAH*, they are under a curse!"

50 Nicodemus, the man who had gone to *YESHUA* before and was one of them, said to them, 51 "Does our *TORAH* condemn a man before hearing from him and finding out what he is doing?" 52 They replied, "You are not from the Galilee too, are you? Study the *Tanakh*, and see for yourself that no prophet comes from the Galilee!" 53 Then they all left, each one to his own home.

8:1 But *YESHUA* went to the Mount of Olives. 2 At daybreak, He appeared again in the TEMPLE Court, where all the people gathered around Him, and He sat down to teach them. 3 The *TORAH*-Teachers and the Pharisees brought in a woman who had been caught committing adultery and made her stand in the center of the group. 4 Then they said to Him, "*RABBI*, this woman was caught in the very act of committing adultery. 5 Now in our *TORAH*, Moses commanded that such a woman be stoned to death. What do you say about it?" 6 They said this to trap Him, so that they might have ground for bringing charges against Him; but *YESHUA* bent down and began writing in the dust with His Finger. 7 When they kept questioning Him, He straightened up and said to them, "The one of you who is without sin, let him be the first to throw a stone at her." 8 Then He bent down and wrote in the dust again. 9 On hearing this, they began to leave, one by one, the older ones first, until He was left alone, with the woman still there. 10 Standing up, *YESHUA* said to her, "Where are they? Has no one condemned you?" 11 She said, "No one, sir." *YESHUA* said, "Neither do I condemn you. Now go, and do not sin anymore."

12 *YESHUA* spoke to them again: "I Am the Light of the world; whoever follows Me will never walk in darkness but will have the Light which gives Life." 13 So the Pharisees said to Him, "Now you are testifying on Your own behalf; Your Testimony is not valid." 14 *YESHUA* answered them, "Even if I do testify on My behalf, My Testimony is indeed valid; because I know where I come from and where I Am going; but you do not know where I came from or where I Am going. 15 You judge by merely human standards. As for Me, I pass Judgment on no one; 16 but if I were indeed to pass Judgment, My Judgment would be valid; because it is not I alone who judge, but I and the One who sent Me. 17 And even in your *Torah* it is written that the testimony of two people is valid. 18

I Myself testify on My Own behalf, and so does the FATHER who sent Me."

19 They said to Him, "Where is this 'FATHER' of Yours?" *YESHUA* answered, "You know neither Me nor My FATHER; if you knew Me, you would know My FATHER too." 20 He said these things when He was teaching in the TEMPLE Treasury Room; yet no one arrested Him, because His time had not yet come.

21 Again He told them, "I Am going away, and you will look for Me, but you will die in your sin. Where I Am going, you cannot come." 22 The Jews said, "Is He going to commit suicide? Is that what He means when He says, 'Where I Am going, you cannot come'?" 23 *YESHUA* said to them, "You are from below, I Am from above; you are of this world, I Am not of this world. 24 This is why I said to you that you will die in your sins; for if you do not have faith that I Am [who I say I Am], you will die in your sins."

25 At this, they said to Him, "You? Who are you?" *YESHUA* answered, "Just what I have been telling you from the start. 26 There are many things I could say about you, and many judgments I could make. However, the One who sent Me is True; so I say in the world only what I have heard from Him."

27 They did not understand that He was talking to them about the FATHER. 28 So *YESHUA* said, "When you lift up the SON of Man, then you will know that I Am [who I say I Am], and that of Myself I do nothing, but say only what the FATHER has taught Me. 29 Also, the One who sent me is still with Me; He did not leave Me to Myself, because I always do what pleases Him."

30 Many people who heard Him say these things put their faith in Him. 31 So *YESHUA* said to the Jews who had put their faith in Him, "If you obey what I say, then you are really My Disciples, 32 you will know the Truth, and the Truth will set you Free." 33 They answered, "We are the seed of Abraham and have never been slaves to anyone; so what do You mean by saying, 'You will be set Free'?" 34 *YESHUA* answered them, "Yes, indeed! I tell you that everyone who practices sin is a slave of sin. 35 Now a slave does not remain with a family forever, but a son does remain with it forever. 36 So if the SON Frees you, you will really be Free! 37 I know you are the seed of Abraham. Yet you are out to kill Me, because what I Am saying makes no headway in you. 38 I say what My FATHER has shown Me; you do what your father has told you!"

39 They answered him, "Our father is Abraham." *YESHUA* replied, "If you are children of Abraham, then do the things

Abraham did! 40 As it is, you are out to kill Me, a Man who has told you the truth which I heard from *ELOHIM*. Abraham did nothing like that! 41 You are doing the things your father does." "We are not illegitimate children!" They said to him. "We have only one FATHER, *ELOHIM*!" 42 *YESHUA* replied to them, "If *ELOHIM* were your FATHER, you would love Me; because I came out from *ELOHIM*; and now I have arrived here. I did not come on My own; He sent Me. 43 Why do you not understand what I Am saying? Because you cannot bear to listen to My message. 44 You belong to your father, Satan, and you want to carry out your father's desires. From the start he was a murderer, and he has never stood by the Truth, because there is no Truth in him. When he tells a lie, he is speaking in character; because he is a liar; indeed, the inventor of the lie! 45 But as for Me, because I tell the Truth you do not believe Me. 46 Which one of you can show Me where I Am wrong? If I Am telling the Truth, why do you not believe Me? 47 Whoever belongs to *ELOHIM* listens to what *ELOHIM* says; the reason you do not listen is that you do not belong to *ELOHIM*."

48 The Jews answered Him, "Are we not right in saying You are from Samaria and have a *demon*?" 49 *YESHUA* replied, "Me? I have no *demon*. I Am honoring My FATHER. But you

dishonor Me. 50 I Am not seeking praise for Myself. There is One who is seeking it, and He is the Judge. 51 Yes, indeed! I tell you that whoever obeys My Teaching will never see death."

52 The Jews said to Him, "Now we know for sure that You have a *demon*! Abraham died, and so did the prophets; yet You say, 'Whoever obeys My Teaching will never taste death.' 53 Abraham our father died; you are not greater than He, are You? And the prophets also died. Who do You think You are?" 54 *YESHUA* answered, "If I praise Myself, My praise counts for nothing. The One who is praising Me is My FATHER, the very One about whom you keep saying, 'He is our *ELOHIM*.' 55 Now you have not known Him, but I do know Him; indeed, if I were to say that I do not know Him, I would be a liar like you! But I do know Him, and I obey His WORD. 56 Abraham, your father, was glad that he would see My Day; then he saw it and was overjoyed."

57 "Why, you are not yet fifty years old," the Jews replied, "And you have seen Abraham?" 58 *YESHUA* said to them, "Yes, indeed! Before Abraham came into being, I AM!" 59 At this, they picked up stones to throw at Him; but *YESHUA* was hidden and left the TEMPLE Grounds.

9:1 As *YESHUA* passed along, He saw a man blind from birth. 2 His Disciples asked Him, "*RABBI*, who sinned, this man or his parents, to cause him to be born blind?" 3 *YESHUA* answered, "His blindness is due neither to his sin nor to that of his parents; it happened so that *ELOHIM'S* Power might be seen at work in him. 4 As long as it is day, we must keep doing the work of the One who sent Me; the night is coming, when no one can work. 5 While I Am in the world, I Am the Light of the World."

6 Having said this, He spit on the ground, made some mud with the saliva, put the mud on the man's eyes, 7 and said to him, "Go, wash off in the Pool of Siloam" (The name means "sent.") So he went and washed and came away seeing.

8 His neighbors and those who previously had seen him begging said, "Is not this the man who used to sit and beg?" 9 Some said, "yes, he is the one;" while others said, "No, but he looks like him." However, he himself said, "I am the one." 10 "How were your eyes opened?" They asked him. 11 He answered, "The Man called *YESHUA* made mud, put it on my eyes, and told me, 'Go to Siloam and wash!' So I went; and as soon as I had washed, I could see." 12 They said to him,

"Where is He?" and he replied, "I do not know."

13 They took the man who had been blind to the Pharisees. 14 Now the day on which YESHUA had made the mud and opened his eyes was the Sabbath. 15 So the Pharisees asked him again how he had become able to see; and he told them, "He put mud on my eyes, then I washed, and now I can see." 16 At this, some of the Pharisees said, "This Man is not from ELOHIM, because He does not keep the Sabbath." But others said, "How could a man who is a sinner do miracles like these?" And there was a split among them. 17 So once more they spoke to the blind man: "Since you are the one whose eyes He opened, what do you say about Him?" He replied: "He is a Prophet."

18 The Jews, however, were unwilling to believe that he had formerly been blind, but now could see, until they had summoned the man's parents. 19 They asked them, "Is this your son who you say was born blind? How is it that now he can see?" 20 His parents answered, "We know that this is our son and that he was born blind; 21 but how it is that he can see now, we do not know; nor do we know who opened his eyes. Ask him; he is old enough, he can speak for himself!" 22 The parents said this because they were afraid of the Judeans, for the Jews had already agreed that anyone who acknowledged YESHUA as the MESSIAH would be banned from the

Assembly. 23 This is why his parents said, "he is old enough, ask him."

24 So a second time they called the man who had been blind; and they said to him, "Swear to *ELOHIM* that you will tell the truth! We know that this Man is a sinner." 25 He answered, "Whether He is a sinner or not I do not know. One thing I do know: I was blind, now I see." 26 So they said to him, "What did He do to you? How did He open your eyes?" 27 "I already told you," he answered, "And you did not listen. Why do you want to hear it again? Maybe you too want to become His Disciples?" 28 Then they railed at him. "You may be His Disciple," they said, "But we are disciples of Moses! 29 We know that *ELOHIM* has spoken to Moses, but this one, we do not know where He is from!" 30 "What a strange thing," the man answered, "That you do not know where He is from; considering that He opened my eyes! 31 We know that *ELOHIM* does not listen to sinners; but if anyone fears *ELOHIM* and does His Will, *ELOHIM* does listen to him. 32 In all history no one has ever heard of someone opening the eyes of a man born blind. 33 If this Man were not from *ELOHIM*, He could not do a thing!" 34 "Why, you sinner!" they retorted, "Are you lecturing us?" And they threw him out.

35 *YESHUA* heard that they had thrown the man out. He found

him and said, "Do you have faith in the SON of Man?" 36 "Sir," he answered, "Tell me who He is, so that I can have faith in Him." 37 *YESHUA* said to him, "You have seen Him. In fact, He is the One speaking with you now." 38 "LORD, I have faith!" he said, and he kneeled down in front of Him.

39 *YESHUA* said, "It is to Judge that I came into this world, so that those who do not see might see, and those who do see might become blind." 40 Some of the Pharisees nearby heard this and said to Him, "So we are blind too, are we?" 41 *YESHUA* answered them, "If you were blind, you would not be guilty of sin. But since you still say, 'We see,' your guilt remains.

10:1 "Yes, indeed! I tell you, the person who does not enter the sheep-pen through the door, but climbs in some other way, is a thief and a robber. 2 But the One who goes in through the gate is the sheep's own Shepherd. 3 This is the One the gate-keeper admits, and the sheep hear His Voice. He calls His Own Sheep, each one by name, and leads them out. 4 After taking out all that are His Own, He goes on ahead of them; and the sheep follow Him because they recognize His Voice. 5 They never follow a stranger but will run away from him, because strangers' voices are unfamiliar to them."

6 *YESHUA* used this indirect manner of speaking with them, but they did not understand what He was talking to them about. 7 So *YESHUA* said to them again, "yes, indeed! I tell you that I Am the Gate for the sheep. 8 All those who have come before Me have been thieves and robbers, but the sheep did not listen to them. 9 I Am the Gate; if someone enters through Me, he will be safe and will go in and out and find pasture. 10 The thief comes only in order to steal, kill and destroy; I have come so that they may have Life, Life in its fullest measure.

11 "I Am the Good Shepherd. The Good Shepherd lays down His Life for the sheep. 12 The hired hand, since he is not a shepherd and the sheep are not his own, sees the wolf coming, abandons the sheep and runs away. Then the wolf drags them off and scatters them. 13 The hired worker behaves like this because that is all he is, a hired worker; so it does not matter to him what happens to the sheep. 14 I Am the Good Shepherd; I know My Own, and My Own know Me; 15 just as the FATHER knows Me, and I know the FATHER; and I lay down My Life on behalf of the sheep. 16 Also I have other sheep which are not from this pen; I need to bring them, and they will hear My Voice; and there will be One Flock, One Shepherd.

17 "This is why the FATHER loves Me: because I lay down My Life; in order to take it up again! 18 No one takes it away from Me; on the contrary, I lay it down of My Own free will. I have the Power to lay it down, and I have the Power to take it up again. This is what My FATHER Commanded Me to do."

19 Again there was a split among the Jews because of what He said. 20 Many of them said, "He has a *demon!*" and "He is crazy! Why do you listen to him?" 21 Others said, "These are not the deeds of a man who is *demonized*. How can a *demon* open blind people's eyes?"

22 Then came *Chanukkah* in *Yerushalayim*. It was winter, 23 and *YESHUA* was walking around inside the TEMPLE area, in Solomon's Porch. 24 So the Jews surrounded Him and said to Him, "How much longer are you going to keep us in suspense? If you are the MESSIAH, tell us publicly!" 25 *YESHUA* answered them, "I have already told you, and you do not have faith in Me. The works I do in My FATHER'S NAME testify on my behalf, 26 but the reason you do not have faith is that you are not included among My Sheep. 27 My Sheep listen to My Voice, I recognize them, they follow Me, 28 and I give them Eternal Life. They will absolutely never be destroyed, and no one will snatch them from My Hands. 29 My FATHER, who gave them to Me, is greater than all; and no one can snatch

them from the FATHER'S Hands. 30 I and the FATHER are One."

31 Once again the Jews picked up rocks in order to stone Him. 32 *YESHUA* answered them, "You have seen Me do many good deeds that reflect the FATHER'S Power; for which one of these deeds are you stoning Me?" 33 The Jews replied, "We are not stoning you for any good deed, but for blasphemy; because You, who are only a man, are making Yourself out to be *ELOHIM*." 34 *YESHUA* answered them, "Is it not written in your *Torah*, Psalms 82:6 **'I have said, "You people are elohim'?"** 35 If He called *'elohim'* the people to whom the WORD of *ELOHIM* was addressed (and the *Tanakh* cannot be broken), 36 then are you telling the One whom the FATHER set apart as Holy and sent into the world, 'You are committing blasphemy,' just because I said, 'I Am a SON of *ELOHIM*'?

37 If I Am not doing the deeds that reflect My FATHER'S Power, do not have faith in Me. 38 But if I Am, then even if you do not have faith in Me, have faith in the deeds; so that you may understand once and for all that the FATHER is united with Me, and I Am united with the FATHER." 39 One more time they tried to arrest Him, but He slipped out of their hands.

40 He went off again beyond the Jordan, where John had been witnessing *immersions* at first, and stayed there. 41 Many people came to Him and said, "John performed no miracles, but everything John said about this Man was true." 42 And many people there put their faith in Him.

11:1 There was a man who had fallen sick. His name was Lazarus, and he came from Bethany, the village where Mary and her sister Martha lived. 2 (This Mary, whose brother Lazarus had become sick, is the one who poured perfume on the LORD and wiped His Feet with her hair.) 3 So the sisters sent a message to *YESHUA*, "LORD, the man you love is sick." 4 On hearing it, He said, "This sickness will not end in death. No, it is for *ELOHIM'S* Glory, so that the SON of *ELOHIM* may receive Glory through it."

5 *YESHUA* loved Martha and her sister and Lazarus; 6 so when He heard he was sick, first He stayed where He was two more days; 7 then, after this, He said to the disciples, "Let us go back to Judea." 8 The disciples replied, "*RABBI*! Just a short while ago the Jews were out to stone You; and You want to go back there?" 9 *YESHUA* answered, "Are not there twelve hours of daylight? If a person walks during daylight, he does not

stumble; because he sees the Light of this World. 10 But if a person walks at night, he does stumble; because he has no Light with him."

11 *YESHUA* said these things, and afterwards He said to the disciples, "Our friend Lazarus has gone to sleep; but I Am going in order to wake him up." 12 The disciples said to Him, "LORD, if he has gone to sleep, he will get better." 13 Now *YESHUA* had used the phrase to speak about Lazarus's death, but they thought He had been talking literally about sleep. 14 So *YESHUA* told them in plain language, "Lazarus has died. 15 And for your sakes, I Am glad that I was not there, so that you may come to have faith. But let us go to him." 16 Then Thomas (the name means "Twin") said to his fellow disciples, "Yes, we should go, so that we can die with Him!"

17 On arrival, *YESHUA* found that Lazarus had already been in the tomb for four days. 18 Now Bethany was about two miles from *Yerushalayim*, 19 and many of the Jews had come to Martha and Mary in order to comfort them at the loss of their brother. 20 So when Martha heard that *YESHUA* was coming, she went out to meet Him; but Mary continued sitting *shiv'ah* in the house.

21 Martha said to *YESHUA*, "LORD, if you had been here, my

brother would not have died. 22 Even now I know that whatever you ask of *ELOHIM*, *ELOHIM* will give You." 23 *YESHUA* said to her, "Your brother will rise again." 24 Martha said, "I know that he will rise again at the Resurrection in the Last Days." 25 *YESHUA* said to her, "I Am the Resurrection and the Life! Whoever puts his faith in Me will live, even if he dies; 26 and everyone living and having faith in Me will never die. Do you believe this?" 27 She said to Him, "Yes, LORD, I believe that you are the MESSIAH, the SON of *ELOHIM*, the One coming into the world."

28 After saying this, she went off and secretly called Mary, her sister: "The *RABBI* is here and is calling for you." 29 When she heard this, she jumped up and went to Him. 30 *YESHUA* had not yet come into the village but was still where Martha had met Him; 31 so when the Jews who had been with Mary in the house comforting her saw her get up quickly and go out, they followed her, thinking she was going to the tomb to mourn there.

32 When Mary came to where *YESHUA* was and saw Him, she fell at His Feet and said to Him, "LORD, if You had been here, my brother would not have died." 33 When *YESHUA* saw her crying, and also the Jews who came with her crying, He was deeply moved and also troubled. 34 He said, "Where have you

buried him?" They said, "LORD, come and see." 35 *YESHUA* cried; 36 so the Jews there said, "See how He loved him!" 37 But some of them said, "He opened the blind man's eyes. Could not He have kept this one from dying?"

38 *YESHUA*, again deeply moved, came to the tomb. It was a cave, and a stone was lying in front of the entrance. 39 *YESHUA* said, "Take the stone away!" Martha, the sister of the dead man, said to *YESHUA*, "By now his body must smell, for it has been four days since he died!" 40 *YESHUA* said to her, "Did I not tell you that if you, having faith, you will see the Glory of *ELOHIM*?" 41 So they removed the stone. *YESHUA* looked upward and said, "FATHER, I thank You that You have heard Me. 42 I Myself know that You always hear Me, but I say this because of the crowd standing around, so that they may believe that You have sent Me." 43 Having said this, He shouted, "Lazarus! Come out!" 44 The man who had been dead came out, his hands and feet wrapped in strips of linen and his face covered with a cloth. *YESHUA* said to them, "Unwrap him, and let him go!" 45 At this, many of the Jews who had come to visit Mary, and had seen what *YESHUA* had done, had faith in Him.

46 But some of them went off to the Pharisees and told them what He had done. 47 So the head Priests and the Pharisees

called a meeting of the *Sanhedrin* and said, "What are we going to do? For this Man is performing many miracles. 48 If we let Him keep going on this way, everyone will have faith in Him, and the Romans will come and destroy both the TEMPLE and the nation." 49 But one of them, Caiaphas, who was the High Priest that year, said to them, "You people do not know anything! 50 You do not see that it is better for you if one man dies on behalf of the people, so that the whole nation would not be destroyed." 51 Now he did not speak this way on his own initiative; rather, since he was The High Priest that year, he was prophesying that *YESHUA* was about to die on behalf of the nation, 52 and not for the nation alone, but so that He might gather into one the scattered Children of *ELOHIM*.

53 From that day on, they made plans to have Him put to death. 54 Therefore *YESHUA* no longer walked around openly among the Jews but went away from there into the region near the wilderness, to a town called Ephraim, and stayed there with His Disciples.

55 The *Appointed Time* for the festival of Passover was near, and many people went up from the country to *Yerushalayim* to perform the purification ceremony prior to Passover. 56 They were looking for *YESHUA*, and as they stood in the TEMPLE Courts they said to each other, "What do you think? That He

simply would not come to the festival?" 57 Moreover, the head Priest and the Pharisees had given orders that anyone knowing *YESHUA'S* whereabouts should inform them, so that they could have Him arrested.

12:1 Six days before Passover, *YESHUA* came to Bethany, where Lazarus lived, the man *YESHUA* had raised from the dead; 2 so they gave a dinner there in His honor. Martha served the meal, and Lazarus was among those at the table with Him. 3 Mary took a whole pint of pure oil of spikenard, which is very expensive, poured it on *YESHUA'S* Feet and wiped His Feet with her hair, so that the house was filled with the fragrance of the perfume. 4 But one of the Disciples, Judah from Iscariot, the one who was about to betray Him, said, 5 "This perfume is worth a year's wages! Why was not it sold and the money given to the poor?" 6 Now he said this not out of concern for the poor, but because he was a thief; he was in charge of the common purse and used to steal from it. 7 *YESHUA* said, "Leave her alone! She kept this for the day of My burial. 8 You always have the poor among you, but you will not always have Me."

9 A large crowd of Jews learned that He was there; and they

came not only because of *YESHUA*, but also so that they could see Lazarus, whom He had raised from the dead. 10 The head Priests then decided to do away with Lazarus too, 11 since it was because of him that large numbers of the Jews were leaving their leaders and putting their faith in *YESHUA*.

12 The next day, the large crowd that had come for the festival heard that *YESHUA* was on His way into *Yerushalayim*. 13 They took palm branches and went out to meet Him, shouting, Psalms 118:25 **"Deliver us!"** Psalms 118:26 **"Blessed is He who comes in the name of *ADONAI*,** the KING of *Yisrael*!" 14 After finding a donkey colt, *YESHUA* mounted it, just as the *Tanakh* says- Zechariah 9:9, 15 **"Daughter of Zion, do not be afraid! Look! Your KING is coming, sitting on a donkey's colt."**

[Witnesses: Matthew 21:4-11 "This happened in order to fulfill what had been spoken through the prophet, 5 'Say to the daughter of Zion,' **"Look! Your KING is coming to you, riding humbly on a donkey, and on a colt, the offspring of a beast of burden!"** So the disciples went and did a *YESHUA* had directed them. 7 They brought the donkey and the colt and put their robes on them, and *YESHUA* sat on them. 8 Crowds of people carpeted the road with their clothing, while others cut branches from trees and spread them on the road. 9 The crowds ahead of Him and behind shouted, **'Please! Deliver us!'** to the SON of David; **'Blessed is he who comes in the name of ADONAI!'** 'You in the highest heaven! Please! Deliver us!' When He entered *Yerushalayim*, the whole city was stirred. 'Who is this?' they asked. 11 And the crowds answered, 'This is *YESHUA*, the PROPHET from Nazareth in the Galilee." Mark 11:7-10 and Luke 19:32-38 repeat Matthew.]

12:16 His Disciples did not understand at first; but after *YESHUA* had been Glorified, then they remembered that the *Tanakh* said this about Him, and that they had done this for Him. 17 The group that had been with Him when He called Lazarus out of the tomb and raised him from the dead had been telling about it. 18 It was because of this too that the crowd came out to meet Him, they had heard that He had performed this miracle. 19 The Pharisees said to each other, "Look, you are getting nowhere! Why, the whole world has gone after Him!"

20 Among those who went up to worship at the festival were some Greek-speaking Jews. 21 They approached Philip, the

one from Bethsaida in the Galilee, with a request. "Sir," they said, "We would like to see YESHUA." 22 Philip came and told Andrew; then Andrew and Philip went and told YESHUA." 23 YESHUA gave them this answer: "The time has come for the SON of Man to be Glorified. 24 Yes, indeed! I tell you that unless a grain of wheat that falls to the ground dies, it stays just a grain; but it dies, it produces a big harvest. 25 He who loves his life loses it, but he who hates his life in this world will keep it safe right on into Eternal Life! 26 If someone is serving Me, let him follow Me; wherever I Am, My servant will be there too. My FATHER will honor anyone who serves Me.

27 "Now I Am in turmoil. What can I say, 'FATHER, save Me from this hour?' No, it was for this very reason that I have come to this hour. I will say this: 28 'FATHER, Glorify your NAME!'" At this a Voice came out of Heaven, "I have Glorified it before, and I will Glorify it again!" 29 The crowd standing there and hearing it said that it had thundered; others said, "And angel spoke to Him." 30 YESHUA answered, "This voice did not come for My sake but for your. 31 Now is the time for this world to be judged, now the ruler of this world will be expelled. 32 As for Me, when I Am lifted up from the earth, I will draw everyone to Myself." 33 He said this to indicate what kind of death He would die.

34 The crowd answered, "We have learned from the *TORAH* that the MESSIAH remains forever. How is it that you say the SON of Man has to be 'Lifted up?' Who is this 'SON of Man?'" 35 *YESHUA* said to them, "The Light will be with you only a little while longer. Walk while you have the Light, or the dark will overtake you; he who walks in the dark does not know where he is going. 36 While you have the Light, put your faith in the Light, so that you may become People of the Light." *YESHUA* said these things, then went off and kept Himself hidden from them.

37 Even though He had performed so many miracles in their presence, they still did not put their faith in Him, 38 in order that what Isaiah the prophet had said might be fulfilled, Isaiah 53:1 **"ADONAI, who has believed our report? To whom has the arm of *ADONAI* been revealed?"**

39 The reason they could not believe was as Isaiah 6:10 says, 40 **"He has blinded their eyes and hardened their hearts, so that they do not see with their eyes, understand with their hearts, and repent, so that I could heal them."**

41 (Isaiah said these things because he saw the DIVINE PRESENCE of *YESHUA* and spoke about Him.) 42 Nevertheless, many of the leaders did have faith in Him; but

because of the Pharisees they did not say so openly, out of fear of being banned from the Assembly 43 for they loved praise from other people more than praise from *ELOHIM*.

44 *YESHUA* declared publicly, "Those who put their faith in Me are trusting not merely in Me, but in the One who sent Me. 45 Also those who see Me see the One who sent Me. 46 I have come as a Light into the world, so that everyone who has faith in Me might not remain in the dark. 47 If anyone hears what I Am saying and does not observe it, I do not judge him; for I did not come to judge the world, but to save the world. 48 Those who reject Me and do not accept what I say have a judge; the WORD which I have spoken will judge them in the Last Days. 49. For I have not spoken on My Own initiative, but the FATHER who sent Me has given Me a Command, namely, what to say and how to say it. 50 And I know that His Command is Eternal Life. So what I say is simply what the FATHER has told Me to say."

Passover *Seder*

13:1 It was just before the festival of Passover, and *YESHUA* knew that the time had come for Him to pass from this world to the FATHER. Having loved His Own people in the world, He loved them to the end. 2 They were at supper, and the Adversary had already put the desire to betray Him into the heart of Judah Son of Simon from Iscariot. 3 *YESHUA* was aware that the FATHER had put everything in His Power, and that He had come from *ELOHIM* and was returning to *ELOHIM*. 4 So He rose from the table, removed His outer garments and wrapped a towel around His Waist. 5 Then He poured some water into a basin and began to wash the feet of the disciples and wipe them off with the towel wrapped around Him.

6 He came to Simon Peter, who said to Him, "LORD! You are washing my feet?" 7 *YESHUA* answered him, "You do not understand yet what I am doing, but in time you will understand." 8 "No!" said Peter, "You will never wash my feet!" *YESHUA* answered him, "If I do not wash you, you have

no share with Me." 9 "LORD," Simon Peter replied, "Not only my feet, but my hands and head too!" 10 *YESHUA* said to him, "A man who has had a bath does not need to wash, except his feet, his body is already clean. And you people are clean, but not all of you." 11 (He knew who was betraying Him; this is why He said, "Not all of you are clean.")

12 After He had washed their feet, taken back His clothes and returned to the table, He said to them, "Do you understand what I have done to you? 13 You call me '*RABBI*' and 'LORD,' and you are right, because I Am. 14 Now if I, the LORD and *RABBI*, have washed your feet, you also should wash each other's feet. 15 For I have set an example for you, so that you may do as I have done to you. 16 Yes, indeed! I tell you, a slave is not greater than his master, nor is an emissary greater than the one who sent him. 17 If you know these things, you will be blessed if you do them.

18 "I Am not talking to all of you, I know which ones I have chosen. But the Words of the *Tanakh* must be fulfilled that say, Psalms 41:10(9) **'The one eating My Bread has turned against Me.'** 19 I Am telling you now, before it happens; so that when it does happen, you may believe that I Am [who I say I Am]. 20 Yes, indeed! I tell you that a person who receives someone I send receives Me, and that anyone who

receives Me receives the One who sent Me."

21 After saying this, *YESHUA*, in deep anguish of Spirit, declared, "Yes, indeed! I tell you that one of you will betray Me." 22 The disciples stared at one another, totally mystified, whom could He mean? 23 One of His Disciples, the one *YESHUA* particularly loved, was reclining close beside Him. 24 So Simon Peter motioned to Him and said, "Ask which one He is talking about." 25 Leaning against *YESHUA'S* chest, He asked *YESHUA*, "LORD, who is it?" 26 *YESHUA* answered, "It is the one to whom I give this piece of unleavened bread after I dip it in the dish." So He dipped the piece of unleavened bread and gave it to Judah Son of Simon from Iscariot. 27 As soon as Judah took the piece of unleavened bread, the Adversary went into him. "What you are doing, do quickly!" *YESHUA* said to him. 28 But no one at the table understood why He had said this to him. 29 Some thought that since Judah was in charge of the common purse, *YESHUA* was telling him, "Buy what we need for the festival," or telling him to give something to the poor. 30 As soon as he had taken the piece of unleavened bread, Judah went out, and it was night.

31 After Judah had left, *YESHUA* said, "Now the SON of Man has been Glorified, and *ELOHIM* has been Glorified in Him. 32 If the SON has Glorified *ELOHIM*, *ELOHIM* will Himself

Glorify the SON, and will do so without delay. 33 Little children, I will be with you only a little longer. You will look for Me; and, as I said to the Jews, 'Where I Am going, you cannot come,' now I say it to you as well.

34 "I Am giving you a New Command: that you keep on loving each other. In the same way that I have loved you, you are also to keep on loving each other. 35 Everyone will know that you are My Disciples by the fact that you have love for each other."

36 Simon Peter said to Him, "LORD, where are you going?" *YESHUA* answered, "Where I Am going, you cannot follow Me now; but you will follow later." 37 "LORD," Peter said to Him, "Why cannot I follow you now? I will lay down my life for You!" 38 *YESHUA* answered, "You will lay down your life for Me? Yes, indeed! I tell you, before the cock crows you will disown Me three times.

14:1 "Do not let yourselves be disturbed. Have faith in *ELOHIM* and faith in Me. 2 In My FATHER'S HOUSE are many places to live. If there were not, I would have told you; because I Am going there to prepare a place for you. 3 Since I Am going and preparing a place for you, I will return to take you with Me; so that where I Am, you may be also. 4 Furthermore, you know where I Am going; and you know the way there."

5 Thomas said to Him, "LORD, we do not know where you are going; so how can we know the way?" 6 *YESHUA* said, "I Am the Way and the Truth and the Life; no one comes to the FATHER except through Me. 7 Because you have known Me, you will also know My FATHER; from now on, you do know Him and in fact, you have seen Him."

8 Philip said to Him, "LORD, show us the FATHER, and it will be enough for us." 9 *YESHUA* replied to him, "Have I been with you so long without your knowing Me, Philip? Whoever has seen Me has seen the FATHER; so how can you say, 'show us the FATHER?' 10 Do you not believe that I Am united with the FATHER, and the FATHER united with Me? What I Am telling you, I Am not saying on My own initiative; the FATHER living in Me is doing His own works. 11 Have faith in Me, that I Am united with the FATHER, and the FATHER united with Me. But if you cannot, then have faith because of the works themselves. 12 Yes, indeed! I tell you that whoever has faith in Me will also do the works I do! Indeed, he will do greater ones, because I Am going to the FATHER. 13 In fact, whatever you ask for in My Name, I will

do; so that the FATHER may be glorified in the SON. 14 If you ask Me for something in My Name, I will do it.

15 "If you love Me, you will keep My Commands; (*TORAH*) 16 and I will ask the FATHER, and He will give you another Comforting Counselor like Me, the Spirit of Truth, to be with you forever. 17 The world cannot receive Her, because it neither sees nor knows Her. You know Her, because She is staying with you and will be united with you. 18 I will not leave you orphans, I Am coming to you. 19 In just a little while, the world will no longer see Me; but you will see Me. Because I live, you too will live. 20 When that day comes, you will know that I Am united with My FATHER, and you with Me, and I with you. 21 Whoever has My Commands (*TORAH*) and keeps them is the one who loves Me, and the one who loves Me will be loved by My FATHER, and I will love him and reveal Myself to him."

22 Judah (not the one from Iscariot) said to Him, "What has happened, LORD, that You are about to reveal Yourself to us and not to the world?" 23 *YESHUA* answered him, "If someone loves Me, he will keep My WORD; and My FATHER will love him, and We will come to him and make Our Home with him. 24 Someone who does not love Me does not keep My WORDS, and the WORD you are hearing is not My Own but

that of the FATHER who sent Me.

25 "I have told you these things while I Am still with you. 26 But the Counselor, the *HOLY SPIRIT*, whom the FATHER will send in My Name, will teach you everything; that is, She will remind you of everything I have said to you.

27 "What I Am leaving you with is Peace and I Am giving you My Peace. I do not give the way the world gives. Do not let yourselves be upset or frightened. 28 You heard Me tell you, 'I Am leaving, and I will come back to you.' If you loved Me, you would have been glad that I Am going to the FATHER; because the FATHER is greater than I. 29 "Also, I have said it to you now, before it happens; so that when it does happen, you have faith.

30 "I will not be talking with you much longer, because the ruler of this world is coming. He has no claim on Me; 31 rather, this is happening so that the world may know that I love the FATHER, and that I do as the FATHER has commanded Me. "Get up! Let's get going!

15:1 "I Am the real Vine, and My FATHER is the Gardener. 2 Every branch which is part of Me but fails to bear fruit, He cuts off; and every branch that does bear fruit, He prunes, so that it may bear more fruit. 3 Right now, because of the WORD which I have spoken to you, you are pruned. 4 Stay united with Me, as I will with you; for just as the branch cannot put forth fruit by itself apart from the vine, so you cannot bear fruit apart from Me.

5 "I Am the Vine and you are the branches. Those who stay united with Me, and I with them, are the ones who bear much fruit; because apart from Me you cannot do a thing. 6 Unless a person remains united with Me, he is thrown away like a branch and dries up. Such branches are gathered and thrown into the fire, where they are burned up.

7 "If you remain united with me, and My WORDS with you, then ask whatever you want, and it will happen for you. 8 This is how My FATHER is Glorified, in your bearing much fruit; this is how you prove to be My Disciples.

9 "Just as My FATHER has loved Me, I too have loved you; so stay in My Love. 10 If you keep My Commands, (*TORAH*) you will stay in My Love, just as I have kept My FATHER'S Commands and stay in His Love. 11 I have said this to you so that My joy may be in you, and your joy be complete.

12 "This is My Command that you keep on loving each other just as I have Loved you. 13 No one has greater love than a

person who lays down his life for his friends. 14 You are My Friends, if you do what I Command you. 15 I no longer call you slaves, because a slave does not know what his master is about; but I have called you Friends, because everything I have heard from My FATHER I have made known to you. 16 You did not choose Me, I chose you; and I have commissioned you to go and bear fruit, fruit that will last; so that whatever you ask from the FATHER in My NAME He may give you. 17 This is what I Command you, keep loving each other!

18 "If the world hates you, understand that it hated Me first. 19 If you belonged to the world, the world would have loved its own. But because you do not belong to the world and on the contrary, I have picked you out of the world and therefore the world hates you. 20 Remember what I told you, 'A slave is not greater than his master.' If they persecuted Me, they will persecute you too; if they kept My WORD, they will keep yours too. 21 But they will do all this to you on My account, because they do not know the One who sent Me.

22 "If I had not come and spoken to them, they would not be guilty of sin; but now, they have no excuse for their sin. 23 Whoever hates Me hates the FATHER also. 24 If I had not done in their presence works which no one else ever did, they would not be guilty of sin; but now, they have seen them and

have hated both Me and My FATHER. 25 But this has happened in order to fulfill the words in their *Torah* which read, Psalms 35:19, 69:5 **'They hated Me for no reason at all.'**

26 "When the Counselor comes, whom I will send you from the FATHER; the SPIRIT of Truth, who keeps going out from the FATHER; She will testify on My behalf. 27 And you will testify too, because you have been with Me from the outset.

16:1 "I have told you these things so that you would not be caught by surprise. 2 They will ban you from the Assembly; in fact, the time will come when anyone who kills you will think he is serving *ELOHIM*! 3 They will do these things because they have understood neither the FATHER nor Me. 4 But I have told you this, so that when the time comes for it to happen, you will remember that I told you. I did not tell you this at first, because I was with you. 5 But now I Am going to the One who sent Me. "Not one of you is asking Me, 'Where are you going?' 6 Instead, because I have said these things to you, you are overcome with grief. 7 But I tell you the *T*ruth, it is to your advantage that I go away; for if I do not go away, the Comforting Counselor will not come to you. However, if I do go, I will send Her to you.

8 "When She comes, She will show that the world is wrong about sin, about righteousness and about judgment; 9 about sin, in that people do not put their faith in Me; 10 about righteousness, in that I Am going to the FATHER and you will no longer see Me; 11 about judgment, in that the ruler of this world has been judged.

12 "I still have many things to tell you, but you cannot bear them now. 13 However, when the SPIRIT of Truth comes, She will guide you into all Truth; for She will not speak on Her Own initiative but will say only what She hears. She will also announce to you the events of the future. 14 She will Glorify Me, because She will receive from what is Mine and announce it to you. 15 Everything the FATHER has is Mine; this is why I said that She receives from what is Mine and will announce it to you.

16 "In a little while, you will see Me no more; then, a little while later, you will see Me." 17 At this, some of the disciples said to one another, "What is this that He is telling us, 'In a little while, you would not see Me; then, a little while later, you will see Me'? and, 'I Am going to the FATHER'?" 18 They went on saying, "What is this 'Little while'? We do not

understand what He is talking about."

19 *YESHUA* knew that they wanted to ask Him, so He said to them, "Are you asking each other what I meant by saying, 'In a little while, you would not see Me; and then, a little while later, you will see Me'? 20 Yes, it is true. I tell you that you will sob and mourn, and the world will rejoice; you will grieve, but your grief will turn to joy. 21 When a woman is giving birth, she is in pain; because her time has come. But when the baby is born, she forgets her suffering out of joy that a child has come into the world. 22 So you do indeed feel grief now, but I Am going to see you again. Then your hearts will be full of joy, and no one will take your joy away from you.

23 "When that day comes, you would not ask anything of Me! Yes, indeed! I tell you that whatever you ask from the FATHER, He will give you in My NAME. 24 Till now you have not asked for anything in My NAME. Keep asking, and you will receive, so that your joy may be complete.

25 "I have said these things to you with the help of illustrations; however, a time is coming when I will no longer speak indirectly but will talk about the FATHER in plain language. 26 When that day comes, you will ask in My NAME. I Am not telling you that I will pray to the FATHER on your

behalf, 27 for the FATHER Himself loves you, because you have loved Me and have believed that I came from *ELOHIM*.

28 "I came from the FATHER and have come into the world; again, I Am leaving the world and returning to the FATHER."

29 The disciples said to him, "Look, You are talking plainly right now, You are not speaking indirectly at all. 30 Now we know that You know everything, and that You do not need to have people put their questions into words. This makes us believe that You came from *ELOHIM*."

31 *YESHUA* answered, "Now you do believe. 32 But a time is coming and indeed it has already come, when you will be scattered, each one looking out for himself; and you will leave Me all alone. Yet I Am not alone; because the FATHER is with Me.

33 "I have said these things to you so that, united with Me, you may have Peace. In the world, you have troubles. But be brave! I have conquered the world!"

17:1 After *YESHUA* had said these things, He looked up toward heaven and said, "FATHER, the time has come. Glorify Your SON, so that the SON may Glorify You and 2 just as You gave Him authority over all mankind, so that He might give

Eternal Life to all those whom You have given Him. 3 And Eternal Life is this: to know You, the One True *ELOHIM*, and Him whom You sent, *YESHUA* the MESSIAH.

4 "I Glorified You on earth by finishing the work You gave Me to do. 5 Now, FATHER, Glorify Me alongside Yourself. Give Me the same Glory I had with You before the world existed.

6 "I made Your NAME known to the people You gave Me out of the world. They were Yours, You gave them to Me, and they have kept Your WORD. 7 Now they know that everything You have given Me is from You, 8 because the WORDS You gave Me I have given to them, and they have received them. They have really come to know that I came from You, and they have come to have faith that you sent Me.

9 "I Am praying for them. I Am not praying for the world, but for those you have given to Me, because they are Yours. 10 Indeed, all I have is Yours, and all You have is Mine, and in them I have been Glorified. 11 Now I Am no longer in the world. They are in the world, but I Am coming to You. HOLY FATHER, guard them by the power of Your NAME, which You have given to Me, so that they may be one, just as We are. 12 When I was with them, I guarded them by the power of Your NAME, which You have given to Me; yes, I kept watch

over them; and not one of them was destroyed (except the one meant for destruction, so that the *Tanakh* might be fulfilled). 13 But now, I Am coming to You; and I say these things while I Am still in the world so that they may have My Joy made complete in themselves.

14 "I have given them Your WORD, and the world hated them, because they do not belong to the world; just as I Myself do not belong to the world. 15 I do not ask You to take them out of the world, but to protect them from the Evil One. 16 They do not belong to the world, just as I do not belong to the world. 17 Set them apart for Holiness by means of the Truth for Your WORD is Truth. 18 Just as You sent Me into the world, I have sent them into the world. 19 On their behalf I Am setting Myself apart for Holiness, so that they too may be set apart for Holiness by means of the Truth.

20 "I pray not only for these, but also for those who will have faith in Me because of their word, 21 that they may all be one. Just as You, FATHER, are united with Me and I with You, I pray that they may be united with Us, so that the world may believe that You sent Me. 22 The Glory which You have given to Me, I have given to them; so that they may be one, just as We are One and 23 I AM united with them and You with Me, so that they may be completely one, and the world thus realize

that You sent Me, and that You have Loved them just as You have Loved Me.

24 "FATHER, I want those You have given Me to be with Me where I Am; so that they may see My GLORY, which You have given Me because You Loved Me before the creation of the world. 25 Righteous FATHER, the world has not known You, but I have known You, and these people have known that You sent Me. 26 I made Your NAME known to them, and I will continue to make it known; so that the Love with which You have Loved Me may be in them, and I Myself may be united with them."

18:1 After *YESHUA* had said all this, He went out with His Disciples across the stream that flows in winter through the Cedron Valley, to a spot where there was a grove of trees; and He and His Disciples went into it. 2 Now Judah, who was betraying Him, also knew the place; because *YESHUA* had often met there with His Disciples. 3 So Judah went there, taking with Him a detachment of Roman soldiers and some TEMPLE Guards provided by the head Priests and the Pharisees; they carried weapons, lanterns and torches. 4 *YESHUA*, who knew everything that was going to happen to

Him, went out and asked them, "Whom do you want?" 5 "*YESHUA* from Nazareth," they answered. He said to them, "I Am." Also standing with them was Judah, the one who was betraying Him. 6 When He said, "I Am," they went backward from Him and fell to the ground. 7 So He inquired of them once more, "Whom do you want?" and they said, "*YESHUA* from Nazareth." 8 "I told you, 'I Am,'" answered *YESHUA*, "So if I Am the one you want, let these others go." 9 This happened so that what He had said might be fulfilled, "I have not lost one of those You gave Me."

10 Then Simon Peter, who had a sword, drew it and struck the slave of The High Priest, cutting off his right ear; the slave's name was Malchus. 11 *YESHUA* said to Peter, "Put your sword back in its scabbard! This is the cup the FATHER has given Me; am I not to drink it?"

12 So the detachment of Roman soldiers and their captain, together with the TEMPLE Guard of the Jews, arrested *YESHUA*, tied Him up, 13 and took Him first to 'Annas, the father-in-law of Caiaphas, who was The High Priest that fateful year. 14 (It was Caiaphas who had advised the Jews that it would be good for one man to die on behalf of the people.) 15 Simon Peter and another disciple followed *YESHUA*. The second disciple was known to The High Priest, and he went

with *YESHUA* into the courtyard of The High Priest; 16 but Peter stood outside by the gate. So the other disciple, the one known to The High Priest, went back out and spoke to the woman on duty at the gate, then brought Peter inside. 17 The woman at the gate said to Peter, "You are one of that Man's Disciples?" He said, "No, I am not." 18 Now the slaves and guards had lit a fire because it was cold, and they were standing around it warming themselves; Peter joined them and stood warming himself too.

19 The High Priest questioned *YESHUA* about His Disciples and about what He taught. 20 *YESHUA* answered, "I have spoken quite openly to everyone; I have always taught in an Assembly or in the TEMPLE where all Jews meet together, and I have said nothing in secret; 21 so why are you questioning Me? Question the ones who heard what I said to them; look, they know what I said." 22 At these words, one of the guards standing by slapped *YESHUA* in the face and said, "This is how You talk to the High Priest?" 23 *YESHUA* answered him, "If I said something wrong, state publicly what was wrong; but if I was right, why are you hitting Me?" 24 So 'Annas sent Him, still tied up, to Caiaphas, The High Priest.

25 Meanwhile, Simon Peter was standing and warming himself. They said to him, "You are also one of His

Disciples?" He denied it, saying, "No, I am not." 26 One of the slaves of The High Priest, a relative of the man whose ear Peter had cut off, said, "Did not I see you with Him in the grove of trees?" 27 So again Peter denied it, and instantly a cock crowed. (Similar to a Town Crier)

28 They led *YESHUA* from Caiaphas to the governor's headquarters. By now it was early morning. They did not enter the headquarters building because they did not want to become ritually defiled and thus unable to eat the Passover meal. 29 So Pilate went outside to them and said, "What charge are you bringing against this Man?" 30 They answered, "If He had not done something wrong, we would not have brought Him to you." 31 Pilate said to them, "You take Him and judge Him according to your own law." The Jews replied, "We do not have the legal power to put anyone to death." 32 This was so that what *YESHUA* had said, about how He was going to die, might be fulfilled.

33 So Pilate went back into the headquarters, called *YESHUA* and said to Him, "Are you the KING of the Jews?" 34 *YESHUA* answered, "Are you asking this on your own, or have other people told you about Me?" 35 Pilate replied, "Am I a Jew? Your own nation and head Priests have handed You over to me; what have You done?" 36 *YESHUA* answered, "My

KINGDOM does not derive its authority from this world's order of things. If it did, My Men would have fought to keep Me from being arrested by the Jews. But My KINGDOM does not come from here." 37 "So then," Pilate said to Him, "You are a KING, after all." *YESHUA* answered, "You say I Am a KING. The reason I have been born, the reason I have come into the world, is to bear witness to the Truth. Every one who belongs to the Truth listens to Me." 38 Pilate asked him, "What is truth?" Having said this, Pilate went outside again to the Jews and told them, "I do not find any case against Him. 39 However, you have a custom that at Passover I set one prisoner free. Do you want me to set free for you the 'KING of the Jews'?" 40 But they yelled back, "No, not this Man but *Bar-Abba*!" (*Yeshua Bar-Abba* was a revolutionary; verses *YESHUA BEN-ABBA*, SON of My FATHER.)

19:1 Pilate then took *YESHUA* and had Him flogged. 2 The soldiers twisted thorn-branches into a crown and placed it on His Head, put a purple robe on Him, 3 and went up to Him, saying over and over, "Hail, 'KING of the Jews'!" and hitting Him in the face.

4 Pilate went outside once more and said to the crowd, "Look, I am bringing Him out to you to get you to understand that I find no case against Him." 5 So *YESHUA* came out, wearing the thorn-branch crown and the purple robe. Pilate said to them, "Look at the Man!" 6 When the head Priests and the TEMPLE Guards saw Him they shouted, "Put Him to death on the *stake*! Put Him to death on the *stake*!" Pilate said to them, "You take Him out yourselves and put Him to death on the *stake*, because I do not find any case against Him." 7 The Jews answered him, "We have a law; according to that law, He ought to be put to death, because He made Himself out to be the SON of ELOHIM." 8 On hearing this, Pilate became even more frightened.

9 He went back into the headquarters and asked *YESHUA*, "Where are You from?" But *YESHUA* did not answer. 10 So Pilate said to Him, "You refuse to speak to me? Do you not understand that it is in my power either to set You free or to have You executed on the *stake*?" 11 *YESHUA* answered, "You would have no power over Me if it had not been given to you from above; this is why the one who handed Me over to you is guilty of a greater sin." 12 On hearing this, Pilate tried to find a

way to set Him free; but the Jews shouted, "If you set this Man free, it means you are not a 'Friend of the Emperor'! Everyone who claims to be a King is opposing the Emperor!" 13 When Pilate heard what they were saying, he brought *YESHUA* outside and sat down on the judge's seat in the place called The Pavement, but in Hebrew, *Gabbatha*; 14 it was about noon on *Preparation Day* for Passover (14th). He said to the Jews, "Here is your KING!" 15 They shouted, "Take Him away! Take Him away! Put Him to death on the *stake*!" Pilate said to them, "You want me to execute your KING on a *stake*?" The head Priests answered, "We have no king but the Emperor." 16 Then Pilate handed *YESHUA* over to them to have Him put to death on the *stake*. So they took charge of *YESHUA*. 17 Carrying the *stake* Himself He went out to the place called Skull (in Aramaic, *Gulgolta*). 18 There they nailed Him to the *stake* along with two others, one on either side, with *YESHUA* in the middle. 19 Pilate also had a notice written and posted on the *stake*; it read,

YESHUA FROM NATZERET ישוע מנצרת

THE KING OF THE JEWS המלך היהודם

20 Many of the *Jews* read this notice, because the place where *YESHUA* was put on the *stake* was close to the city; and it had

been written in Hebrew, in Latin and in Greek. 21 The Jews head Priests therefore said to Pilate, "Do not write, 'The KING of the Jews,' but 'He said, "I Am KING of the Jews."'" 22 Pilate answered, "what I have written, I have written."

23 When the soldiers had nailed *YESHUA* to the *stake,* they took His clothes and divided them into four shares, a share for each soldier, with the under-robe left over. Now the under-robe was seamless, woven in one piece from top to bottom; 24 so they said to one another, "We should not tear it in pieces; let us cast lots for it." This happened in order to fulfill the Words from the *Tanakh,* Psalms 22:19 (18) "They divided My clothes among themselves **and gambled for My Robe."** This is why the soldiers did these things.

25 Nearby *YESHUA'S* execution *stake* stood His Mother, His Mother's sister Mary the wife of Clopas, and Mary from Magdala. 26 When *YESHUA* saw His Mother and the disciple whom He loved standing there, He said to His Mother, "Mother, this is your son." 27 Then He said to the disciple, "This is your mother." And from that time on, the disciple took her into his own house.

28 After this, knowing that all things had accomplished their purpose, *YESHUA,* in order to fulfill the Words of the *Tanakh,*

said, "I Am thirsty." 29 A jar full of cheap sour wine was there; so they soaked a sponge in the wine, coated it with oregano leaves and held it up to His Mouth. 30 After *YESHUA* had taken the wine, He said, "It is accomplished!" And, letting His Head droop, He delivered up His Spirit.

31 It was *Preparation Day*, and the Jews did not want the bodies to remain on the *stake* on the Sabbath, since it was an especially important Sabbath, (First day of Unleavened Bread). So they asked Pilate to have the legs broken and the bodies removed. 32 The soldiers came and broke the legs of the first man who had been put on a *stake* beside *YESHUA*, then the legs of the other one; 33 but when they got to *YESHUA* and saw that He was already dead, they did not break His Legs. 34 However, one of the soldiers stabbed His Side with a spear, and at once Blood and Water flowed out. 35 The man who saw it has testified about it, and his testimony is true. And he knows that he tells the truth, so you too can have faith. 36 For these things happened in order to fulfill this passage of the *Tanakh*: Psalms 34:21 (20); Exodus 12:46; Numbers 9:12 **"Not one of His bones will be broken."** 37 And again, another passage says, Zechariah 12:10 **"They will look at Him whom they have pierced."**

38 After this, Joseph of Arimathea, who was a disciple of

YESHUA, but a secret one out of fear of the Jews, asked Pilate if he could have *YESHUA'S* Body. Pilate gave his consent, so Joseph came and took the Body away. 39 Also Nicodemus, who at first had gone to see *YESHUA* by night, came with some seventy pounds of spices and a mixture of myrrh with aloes. 40 They took *YESHUA'S* Body and wrapped it up in linen sheets with the spices, in keeping with Jewish burial practice. 41 In the vicinity of where He had been executed was a garden, and in the garden was a new tomb in which no one had ever been buried. 42 So, because it was *Preparation Day* for the Jews, and because the tomb was close by, that is where they buried *YESHUA*.

20:1 Early on the *'first day of the week'* (going-out of the Sabbath), while it was still dark, Mary from Magdala went to the tomb and saw that the stone had been removed from the tomb. 2 So she came running to Simon Peter and the other disciple, the one *YESHUA* loved, and said to them, "They have taken the LORD out of the tomb, and we do not know where they have put Him!"

3 Then Peter and the other disciple started for the tomb. 4 They both ran, but the other disciple out ran Peter and reached the

tomb first. 5 Stooping down, he saw the linen burial-sheets lying there but did not go in. 6 Then, following him, Simon Peter arrived, entered the tomb and saw the burial-sheets lying there, 7 also the cloth that had been around His Head, lying not with the sheets but in a separate place and still folded up. 8 Then the other disciple, who had arrived at the tomb first, also went in; he saw, and he had faith. 9 (They had not yet come to understand that the *Tanakh* teaches that the MESSIAH has to rise from the dead.)

10 So the disciples returned home, 11 but Mary stood outside crying. As she cried, she bent down, peered into the tomb, 12 and saw two angels in white sitting where the body of *YESHUA* had been, one at the head and one at the feet. 13 "Why are you crying?" they asked her. "They took my LORD," she said to them, "And I do not know where they have put Him."

14 As she said this, she turned around and saw *YESHUA* standing there, but she did not know it was He. 15 *YESHUA* said to her, "Lady, why are you crying? Whom are you looking for?" Thinking He was the gardener, she said to Him, "Sir, if you are the one who carried Him away, just tell me where you put Him; and I will go and get Him myself." 16 *YESHUA* said to her, "Mary!" Turning, she cried out to Him in Hebrew,

"*Rabbani!*" (that is, "Teacher!") 17 "Stop holding onto Me," *YESHUA* said to her, "Because I have not yet gone back to the FATHER. But go to My Brothers, and tell them that I Am going back to My FATHER and your FATHER, to My *ELOHIM* and your *ELOHIM*." 18 Mary of Magdala went to the disciples with the news that she had seen the LORD and that He had told her this.

19 In the evening that same day, the first day of the week, when the disciples were gathered together behind locked doors out of fear of the Jews, *YESHUA* came, stood in the middle and said, "Peace be upon you!" 20 Having greeted them, He showed them His Hands and His Side. The disciples were overjoyed to see the LORD. 21 "Peace be upon you!" *YESHUA* repeated. "Just as the FATHER sent Me, I Myself am also sending you." 22 Having said this, He breathed on them and said to them, "Receive the HOLY SPIRIT! 23 If you forgive someone's sins, their sins are forgiven; if you hold them, they are held."

24 Now Thomas (the name means "twin"), one of the Twelve, was not with them when *YESHUA* came. 25 When the other disciples told him, "We have seen the LORD," he replied, "Unless I see the nail marks in His Hands, put my finger into the place where the nails were and put my hand into His Side, I

refuse to believe it."

26 A week later His Disciples were once more in the room, and this time Thomas was with them. Although the doors were locked, *YESHUA* came, stood among them and said, "Peace be upon you!" 27 Then He said to Thomas, "Put your finger here, look at My Hands, take your hand and put it into My Side. Do not be lacking in faith, but have faith!" 28 Thomas answered Him, "My LORD and My *ELOHIM*!" 29 *YESHUA* said to him, "Have you faith because you have seen Me? How blessed are those who do not see, but have faith anyway!"

30 In the presence of the disciples *YESHUA* performed many other miracles which have not been recorded in this book. 31 But these which have been recorded are here so that you may have faith that *YESHUA* is the MESSIAH, the SON of *ELOHIM*, and that by this faith you may have Life because of who He is.

21:1 After this, *YESHUA* appeared again to the disciples at Lake Kinneret Here is how it happened: 2 Simon Peter and Thomas (his name means "twin") were together with Nathanael from Cana in the Galilee, the sons of Zebedee, and two other disciples. 3 Simon Peter said, "I am going fishing." They said to him, "We are coming with you." They went and got into the boat, but that night they did not catch anything. 4 However, just as day was breaking, *YESHUA* stood on shore, but the disciples did not know it was He. 5 He said to them, "You do not have any fish, do you?" "No," they answered Him. 6 He said to them, "Throw in your net to right-side and you will catch some." So they threw in their net, and there were so many fish in it that they could not haul it aboard. 7 The disciple *YESHUA* loved said to Peter, "It is the LORD!" On hearing it was the LORD, Simon Peter threw on his coat, because he was stripped for work, and plunged into the lake; 8 but the other disciples followed in the boat, dragging the net full of fish; for they were not far from shore, only about a hundred yards. 9 When they stepped ashore, they saw a fire of burning coals with a fish on it, and some bread. 10 *YESHUA* said to them, "Bring some of the fish you have just caught." 11 Simon Peter went up and dragged the net ashore. It was full of fish, 153 of them; but even with so many, the net was not torn. 12 *YESHUA* said to them, "Come and have breakfast." None of the disciples dared to ask Him, "Who are You?" They knew it was the LORD. 13 *YESHUA* came, took the bread and gave it to them, and did the same with the fish. 14 This was now the third time *YESHUA* had appeared to the disciples after being raised from the dead.

15 After breakfast, *YESHUA* said to Simon Peter, "Simon *Bar-John*, do you love Me more than these?" He replied, "Yes, LORD, You know I am your friend." He said to him, "Feed My Lambs." 16 A second time He said to him, "Simon Son of John, do you love Me?" He replied, "Yes, LORD, You know I am Your friend." He said to him, "Shepherd My Sheep." 17 The third time He said to him, "Simon Son of John, are you My Friend?" Simon was hurt that He questioned him a third time; "Are you My Friend?" So he replied, "LORD, You know everything! You know I am Your Friend!" *YESHUA* said to him, "Feed My Sheep! 18 Yes, indeed! I tell you, when you were younger, you put on your clothes and went where you wanted. But when you grow old, you will stretch out your hands, and someone else will dress you and carry you where you do not want to go." 19 He said this to indicate the kind of death by which Peter would bring glory to *ELOHIM*. Then *YESHUA* said to him, "Follow Me!"

20 Peter turned and saw the disciple *YESHUA* especially loved following behind, the one who had leaned against Him at the supper and had asked, "Who is the one who is betraying You?" 21 On seeing him, Peter said to *YESHUA*, "LORD, what about him?" 22 *YESHUA* said to him, "If I want him to stay on until I

come, what is it to you? You, follow Me!" 23 Therefore the word spread among the brothers that this disciple would not die. However, *YESHUA* did not say he would not die, but simply, "If I want him to stay on until I come, what is it to you?"

24 This one is the disciple who is testifying about these things and who has recorded them. And we know that his testimony is true.

25 But there are also many other things *YESHUA* did; and if they were all to be recorded, I do not think the whole world could contain the books that would have to be written!

One Passover

	Matthew	Mark	Luke
John 2:13b-17	21:12-13	11:11a	19:45-46
John 6:1-13	14:13-21	6:34-44	9:11-17
John 6:16-21	14:22-34	6:45-53	
John 12:12-15	21:4-11	11:7-10	19:32-38
John 13:2	26:20-21A	14:17-18A	22:14-15
John 13:18, 21	26:21B	14:18B	
John 13:26-27	26:23		14:20

GLOSSARY

No "J's or W's" in the Hebrew language!

Abba - my father.

Adar I - twelfth month in the Festival Year.

Adar II - thirteenth month in the Festival Year, only in a leap year, seven leap years in a nineteen year span.

ADONAI - the LORD, but used in *Y'hudaism* in lieu of the Tetragrammaton, (YAD-HEY-VAV-HEY), which is usually rendered in English as "*YAHVEH*," and "*YEHOVAH*."

Alef - first letter of the Hebrew alphabet.

Alef/Tav - refers to YESHUA, similar to the Alpha and Omega; the first and last.

Av - fifth month in the Festival Year.

Azazel - name of a fallen angel.

Bar - son, son of or descendant of.

Baruch - blessed.

Bar-Abba - Barabbas, son of my father, (full name,

Yeshua bar-Abba) criminal released by Pontius Pilate instead of *YESHUA BEN-ABBA* the Messiah.

Ben - son, son of or descendant of.

B'rit - covenant, similar to contracts.

B'rit HaChidaysh - Covenant the Renewed, aka the New Testament. "Renewed" to the Jew and "New" to the Gentile.

Chanukkah - the Feast of Dedication, Festival of Lights, honoring TEMPLE rededication by the Maccabees.

Cheshvan - eighth month in the Festival Year.

David - King of *Yisrael* and ancestor of *YESHUA* the Messiah.

Demon - Niphla - offspring of a fallen angel and mankind, i.e. Goliath of Gath.

Demons - Nephilim - offspring's of a fallen angel and mankind, i.e., Goliath and his brothers of Gath.

Echad - one, unity, unity of one.

ELOHIM - two or three members of the Godhead.

elohim - children of ELOHIM

Elul - sixth month of the Festival Year.

Essene - followers of the Way; *YESHUA* and John

were *Essenes*; different from the Pharisees and *Tz'dukim*. Also, *Sha'ul*, Acts 24:14.

First Day of the Week - starts sundown Saturday evening.

First Fruits - the first day of the week following the first day of Unleavened Bread, starts Saturday evening after the sun sets and when the first fruits of the barley harvest are taken to the TEMPLE.

Halleluyah - Halleluyah, Praise *Yah!*

Immersion - submerging oneself three times facing upstream.

Iyar - second month in the Festival Year.

John the *Immerser* - John the Baptist.

Jubilee - Fiftieth Year, Year of Release.

Kislev - ninth month of the Festival Year.

K'nesiyah - assembly for a sacred purpose; *Yisrael's* Parliament - Knesset.

Malki-Tzedek - Melchizedek, King/Priest, an order of Priesthood.

Mashiach - Messiah, anointed, and anointed one.

Matzah - unleavened bread. The "first day for Unleavened Bread" would be the day on which, when evening comes, the *Seder* is held. First of the three "Pilgrimage Festivals."

Mayim Chayim - Living Waters; Mayim - waters; Chayim - life, lives. *Mikveh* is done in *Mayim Chayim*, flowing water.

Messianic Jews - Messianic Judaism, Jews that believe in the Messiah.

Mikveh - the ritual bath of purification, pool or bath of flowing water (*Mayim Chayim*); facing upstream and submerging yourself three times.

Mitzvah, pl. *mitzvot* - command, commandment; good deed.

Motza'ei-Shabbat - literally, the "going-out of the Sabbath", i.e., Saturday evening after sunset.

Nisan - first month in the Festival Year.

Omer - sheaf of barley.

Pesach - Passover.

Pesach Seder - Passover meal eaten at the dawning of the fifteenth.

Pilgrimage Feasts - Unleavened Bread, *Shavu'ot*/Pentecost, *and* Tabernacle.

Preparation Day - leaven is removed and the Passover lamb is slaughtered; the day before the Feast of Unleavened Bread, the fourteenth of *Nisan*; Friday, the day before the Sabbath.

Qumran - the area where the "Dead Sea Scrolls" were found and where the Essenes lived.

Rabbi - teacher; in modern *Y'hudaism* a *rabbi* is someone ordained to determine *halakhah* (Jewish law) to judge, and to teach *Torah*.

Rosh Chodesh - the festival, celebrating the beginning of each lunar month.

Rosh HaShanah - head of the year - New Year and Feast of Shofars.

Sabbatical - every seven years times seven = 49 years in a 50 year Yovel cycle.

Sanhedrin - Jewish religious court.

Satan - Adversary, i.e., the Devil. In the *Tanakh* he is described specifically at Job 1–2 and by implication in Isaiah 14:11–15, Ezekiel 28, and Matthew 4:1-11.

Seder - order; the ceremonial evening meal with which Passover begins in Jewish homes.

Shabbat, pl. *Shabbatot* - Sabbath, Friday evening after sundown to Saturday evening at sundown.

Shavu'ot - the Feast of Weeks, since it comes seven

weeks after Passover; also called Pentecost since one counts 50 days after First Fruits. Second of the three "pilgrimage festivals", the other two are Passover and Tabernacle.

Shevat - eleventh month in the Festival Year.

Shivʻah - seven. After the burial of a father, mother, brother, sister, son, daughter or spouse a Jewish mourner remains at home for seven days; this custom is called "sitting *shivʻah*".

Sh'ma Yisrael, Adonai Eloheinu, Adonai Echad - "Hear, O *Yisrael*, the LORD your *ELOHIM*, the LORD is One" (Deuteronomy 6:4).

Shofar - ram's horn; often rendered as "trumpet".

Sivan - third month in the Festival Year.

613 Levitical Laws - includes the Ten Commandments plus 603 more Laws. Not all 613 Laws pertain to anyone person. Some are for the priest only, some for men only, and some are for women only.

Stake - cross.

Sukkot - the Feast of Booths (Tabernacles), it is the third of the three "Pilgrimage Festivals".

Talmud - Jewish commentary on *TORAH*

Tammuz - fourth month in the Festival Year.

Tanakh - acronym formed from the first letters of the three parts of the Hebrew Bible: *TORAH* ("Teaching": the Five Books of Moses or Pentateuch - Genesis, Exodus, Leviticus, Numbers, Deuteronomy); *Nevi'im* ("Prophets": the historical books [Joshua, Judges, Samuel and Kings], the three Major Prophets [Isaiah, Jeremiah, Ezekiel], and the twelve Minor Prophets); and *K'tuvim* ("Writings": Psalms, Proverbs, Job, the Five Scrolls [Song of Songs, Ruth, Esther, Lamentations, Ecclesiastes], Daniel, Ezra-Nehemiah and Chronicles). Hence, the Old Testament. Rendered "scripture" or "it is written" in most translations. The reason the New Testament writers cite the *Tanakh* so frequently is that they understand it as *ELOHIM'S* authoritative WORD to mankind. Mt 4:4+.

Tevet - tenth month in the Festival Year.

Tishri - seventh month in the Festival Year.

TORAH - first five books of the Bible, teaching or

instructions.

Torah - commentary on *TORAH*, including the Prophets, the Writings, *Yerushalayim and Babylonian Talmuds.*

YAHVEH - YESHUA, one member of the Godhead.

YAHVEH'S Appointed Times - the Sabbath, Passover/Unleavened Bread, Omer, Shavu'ot, Rosh HaShanah, Yom Kippur, and Sukkot. Leviticus 23:1-44.

Yerushalayim - Jerusalem.

Yeshivah - Jewish religious school. Ac 19:9.

Yeshua bar-Abba - Barabbas, released from prison and sent to Azazel in the wilderness.

YESHUA - BEN-ELOHIM, YAHVEH.

YESHUA BEN-ABBA - JESUS SON of My FATHER.

YESHUA BEN-YOSEF - JESUS SON of JOSEPH.

Y'hudaism - the life style of living *TORAH* observant.

Yisrael - Israel.

Yom-Kippur - the Day of Atonement, tenth of *Tishri*.

REFERENCES

The Stones Tanakh, by Irving I. Stone

Hebrew Gospel of Matthew, by George Howard

The New Testament from the Ancient Eastern Text, by George M. Lamsa

The Complete Jewish Bible, by David H. Stern

The Dake's Annotated Reference Bible, by Finis Jennings Dake

Dictionary of the Targumim, the Talmud Babli and Yerushalmi, and the Midrashic Literature, by Marcus Jastrow

Strong's Exhaustive Concordance of the Bible, James Strong

Mishlei (Proverbs) Translation and Commentary by *Rabbi* Eliezer Ginsburg

ABOUT THE AUTHOR

My great-grandparents, Herman Robert Rothenberger and his wife Helena (Schmidt) came to the United States in 1884 from Saxony, Germany. They came to Cairo, Illinois and then later settled in Portland, Oregon.

I was born in Portland, Oregon in 1953 and lived most of my life in the Willamette Valley. Married my second wife Marilyn, in 1979; she had two sons and I had one daughter; later, we had two more daughters and one more son.

My trade has been mostly in the Metal Fabrication Industry, building and repairing wood related machinery. In 1997 I started a contracting company which, also included Structural Steel fabrication and Installation.

I was raised a Catholic and when I turned 18 I left the Catholic Church. I had two reasons for leaving: first, I was not living a religious lifestyle and second, there was this thing I heard about and witnessed that the "First born son" would enter the priesthood. Not for me, so I thought. When I met my second wife I told her "You will never get me in church!"

We got married and bought our first home in Gervais, Oregon. Shortly after, I lost my job, the kids started going to church with the neighbors, and then my wife. Not long after this, I was offered a job working with one of the members of this church; it was great working with Christians! I accepted Jesus as my savoir and my lifestyle began to change.

Later, Marilyn and I were introduced to the Jewishness of the Bible and to Judaism. Marilyn and I accepted this new lifestyle and moved to Colorado to continue studying with Dutch & Rita (our neighbors from Gervais, OR) and to live this new lifestyle. I now study and teach TORAH! YESHUA is TORAH; TORAH is Life! This book is part of that study. Showing how YESHUA lived and died within the framework of TORAH; YESHUA, the author of TORAH.

Leonard Mathew Rothenberger, Jr.

www.ingramcontent.com/pod-product-compliance
Lightning Source LLC
Chambersburg PA
CBHW071452040426
42444CB00008B/1301